I0095945

How to Catch Fish

EARLY PRAISE FOR HOW TO CATCH FISH

I've known Dennis for over 20 years, both from his stories published in Bay Weekly, and through fishing with him on a regular basis. Dennis has proved to be a true Chesapeake Bay sportsman. Always willing to give his opinion and expert advice, agree or disagree, but always honestly. His stories and fishing expertise have proven to be a positive influence on the Chesapeake and have made a difference.

Thanks for republishing his many stories and expert fishing techniques.

—Capt. Frank Tuma

Teach a man to fish and he will eat for a lifetime. Give a woman this book and she'll do it faster. I fell for this book hook, line and sinker.

—M. D. Johnson
author of The ISIS Project Series

How to Catch Fish

52 Lessons from 50 Years
of Angling on the Chesapeake

By Dennis Doyle
Bay Weekly's Sporting Life Columnist

How to Catch Fish
by Dennis Doyle

Copyright 2023
by Dennis Doyle
All Rights Reserved

Editor
Sandra Olivetti Martin
New Bay Books
Fairhaven, Maryland
NewBayBooks@gmail.com

Cover Design by Suzanne Shelden

All photos courtesy of the Banker-Doyle family.
Vintage fish illustrations from Dover Pictorial Archive
Animal Illustrations book and from www.shutterstock.com.
Instructive and aerial illustrations by Deborah Banker.

Interior design by Suzanne Shelden
Shelden Studios
Prince Frederick, Maryland
sheldenstudios@comcast.net

A note on type: cover and section heads are set in Above The Sky;
paragraph text is set in Garamond Premier Pro

Library of Congress
Cataloging-in-Publication Data

ISBN: 979-8-9882998-1-3

Printed in the United States of America
First Edition

I dedicate this collection of my columns to my sons John, Harrison and Robert, who are pursuing lives far more adventurous in their own ways than mine was. I wish them all the luck that I enjoyed plus any more that they may need. Every generation seems to face greater challenges than those of the past.

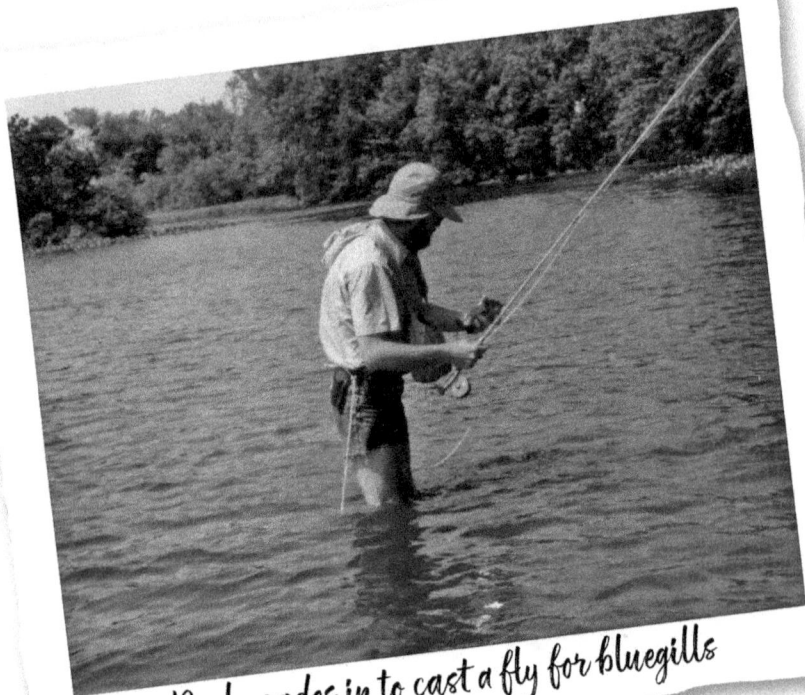

Doyle wades in to cast a fly for bluegills

FOREWORD

By Deborah Banker

It was our third date. A sunny warm spring Saturday. Dennis said "Would you like to try fly fishing? I have a nice little spot on the Eastern Shore."

I was in love. Here was a man completely different from any I had previously met. He cooked, fished and hunted, and I wanted very much to get to know him better.

Yes I replied enthusiastically, *what do I need?*

"Just yourself. We might do a little wading, so shoes that can get wet."

So I appeared in cut-offs, a T-shirt and a pair of old sneakers. We left early Saturday morning on a spring day and drove to the Eastern Shore, then north towards one of Dennis' favorite fishing spots. It was a small lake with a shallow falls at one end and was surrounded with brush and trees. It was beautifully clear day, and the lake looked promising to this novice.

As we unpacked our gear from the car I asked where we would be fishing. Dennis pointed across the lake to the far side. He explained that we would walk across the top of the falls and around the edge to get to the right spot, and then we would wade in. He had previously given me a few fly fishing lessons in the back yard so I had a loose idea of the process and the casting technique.

So we grabbed the gear and headed off. It was easy getting across the falls, but when we reached the far shore, the brush became very dense and the berry bushes closed in on us. It was slow and arduous, but we eventually made it through to a nice clearing by the edge of the lake.

We could see and hear splashes as the spawning fish jumped. The water was clear. Dennis and I slowly and carefully waded in as not to spook the bluegills. He showed me what the spawning beds looked like and how to spot the fish under the water. We spread out so that I didn't hook him with my beginner fly-casting moves.

Almost immediately I hooked a fish. Dennis had the netted bag around his waist, so he came closer to show me how to remove the fly from the fish's mouth and slide the beautiful orange-blue fish into the bag. I was completely obsessed after that first catch. Dennis gave me my own bag to hold the fish I caught, and as we both cast and caught more fish, he wandered off a bit, leaving me a little space to discover the joy of the sport on my own.

Time stopped as I found my rhythm and became lost in the water, the movement of casting the fly and catching the fish. I was in heaven.

After a while, Dennis moseyed back to check on my progress. I was so excited to tell him how many fish I had caught. As I reached back to raise my bag out of the water, I found that it was empty as it had a big hole in it. I accused him of giving me that one on purpose, but with a twinkle in his eye he assured me he didn't see the hole.

He stayed close and started casting, and I bristled at his proximity. He said "Can I fish here next to you?" And I answered *Heck no, you go find your own spot!*

He later told me that was the moment he fell in love with me. As did I. It was the best day fishing I have ever had, a perfect moment when all elements came together for a magical experience.

We took home a full cooler of fish that day. After cleaning and filleting them, we ate a delicious feast topped off with silver queen corn, fresh tomatoes and champagne.

It was an auspicious beginning of a wonderful life together.

Coastland Times 7/25/78 Safe Return

RESCUED BY Coast Guard units, four of the group shown above were happy to touch land again after drifting 120 miles out into the ocean. Dennis Doyle, Michael Kelly, Randy Sted and eight-year-old Woff Mains of Washington, D. C. are shown at the Hatteras Inlet Coast Guard Station shortly after their return to the base by Coast Guard helicopter. On hand to greet the foursome were fiancee and Chief Griffin of the Hatteras Inlet Station.

Dennis Doyle

DIE-HARD FISHERMAN

A party of us—fishermen Michael Kelly and Randy Steck, a couple of girlfriends and a boy—had trailered Dennis Doyle's boat, a center-console 17-foot Mako, to Cape Hatteras for three-days of offshore fishing. Morning of our last day dawned overcast, and there were small craft warnings. Seas were rough, but the wind was offshore.

"The big boats are going out so we will, too," Dennis says, "It isn't supposed to get bad until 1 o'clock. When the big boats turn around to come in, then we will follow."

Out in the Gulf Stream, fishing a weed line, we are surrounded by a school of dolphin fish. We're nailing them, and I'm hanging off the side of the boat trying to gaff one out of the water. There are also big tuna, but we can't get close to them before the dolphin are all over our baits. It's a lovely day with no sign of bad weather, yet.

We're fishing and we're catching, but the chop is getting worse and the bilge pump chugging, when the engine stops. Everybody looks to the captain, who is equally puzzled. "It's been really damp and drizzling, probably a plug has been fouled. Let's change plugs."

When we try the motor again, nothing.

Meanwhile, the ocean is getting much rougher. By now it is mid-morning. We stare at each other, and together we look at Dennis and ask, "What do we do now?"

"Give it time," he says. "I've never had a problem before."

We haven't given it much time when the bigger boats start turning back to shore. Dennis grabs the flare gun and fires three or four flares but they don't see the signals and we eventually give up, hoping that if they'd seen us they had notified someone. That leaves us, the three of us men, a little more rattled. Especially because our fourth passenger, Norman Mains, who we call Wolfie, is 8 years old.

We have a radio, but it had broken down the day before and remained useless. We have no supplies beyond a half bottle of Diet Rite soda, one banana, and fish boxes full of wahoo, blackfin tuna and dolphin fish.

Now what?

The storm hits. Full gale. Sixty mile-per-hour winds. The sea is turmoil, like taking an egg beater and churning. And it's blowing. Luckily it is blowing in the same direction as the Gulf Stream. The Gulf Stream moves at 4 or 5 knots, and with the wind blowing in the same direction, the seas are high and rolling, not crashing. We ride up 15 to 20 feet and then crash down the other side of the waves. As soon as we hit the bottom of the trough, we start bailing. Thinking that we just might capsize, we jettison our dead fish.

For a full afternoon into night, that's how we ride the waves.

Night is the worst. There is lightning, and as each flash lights up the ocean we can see how angry the ocean is and how big the swells are. Somebody says, "Oh shit how are we going to ride this one out?"

It's the middle of July, but it is cold. Randy and Mike are wearing T-shirts and shorts. Dennis holds Wolfie against his chest and zips up his foul weather coat over both of them.

In the night, bailing water, we see a wall of lights and we think "what in the hell is this?"

It is a freighter, close to us, very close, about 100 yards. Dennis gets out the flares, Bam! Bam! He fires two or three into the stormy sky. We're sure they are going to see us. We are getting saved here. Then Dennis yells, "Look out! Here comes the wake. This one could get us. Get ready."

When the swell from the freighter hits us, everybody rocks to the other side of the boat, trying to keep it upright, and we get through it.

It was very close, and we are close to despair. The charter boats hadn't looked at us, and the freighter didn't look at us, either, despite our distress flares. So we keep battling through the night.

With daybreak, the storm calms down. The sun is bright, the day 90 degrees. We have the great idea to put up some fishing poles and hang clothes from them so we can get a little breeze and start sailing. It doesn't work.

Then we hear it; the loud hum of an airplane engine. The Coast Guard has picked up our emergency position-indicating radio beacon (EPIRB) and sent a C130 out to investigate what that signal is all about.

Dennis grabs the flare gun. We see our salvation drop down out of the low clouds, then go back into the clouds. "It's coming right at us, it's going over the top of us," we yell as the second flare almost hits the plane's wing. The plane stays with us, circling for about a half hour, until a U.S. Coast Guard helicopter arrives.

The copter drops us a radio and asks if we want to come out or wait four more hours for a tow. We are ready to go. They drop another EPIRB to put on the boat so a Buoy Tender can find it and tow it to shore.

Next they drop the basket to hoist us, swinging like a pendulum, from sea level up to the copter. Wolfie goes first, followed by Mike, Randy, and finally Dennis. Up in the copter, the crew gives us their box lunches, with the best bologna sandwiches we ever ate.

The flight back to Hatteras takes an hour and a half. We were 120 miles offshore.

A relieved group of people wait for us when we land: Mike Kelly's girlfriend; Dennis' girlfriend, Ann Mains, who is Wolfie's mother; and a Coast Guard chaplain. Dennis' brother, Bill Doyle, and Ken Adams, who had a small plane and pilot's license, had joined the search in the meantime.

They knew of dangers beyond what we had imagined. Bill reported that he had never seen so many sharks in his life. The Coast Guard had cautioned Ann hours earlier, "You better hope they don't come in now because they'll never get past the breakwater."

Despite it all, we survived. We celebrated that night with big T-bone steaks and all the champagne we could find.

I accompanied Dennis on many fishing and hunting trips in the states and internationally, to Ascension Bay, the Bahamas, Baja, Turks and Caicos chasing permit, tarpon, bonefish and bonita. We have lived adventurous lives driven by the pursuit of challenges in the sport of fishing.

This book comes to you from his half century of fishing adventures on Chesapeake Bay.

— Randy Steck

TABLE OF CONTENTS

Spring

Summer

Autumn

Winter

Spring

March

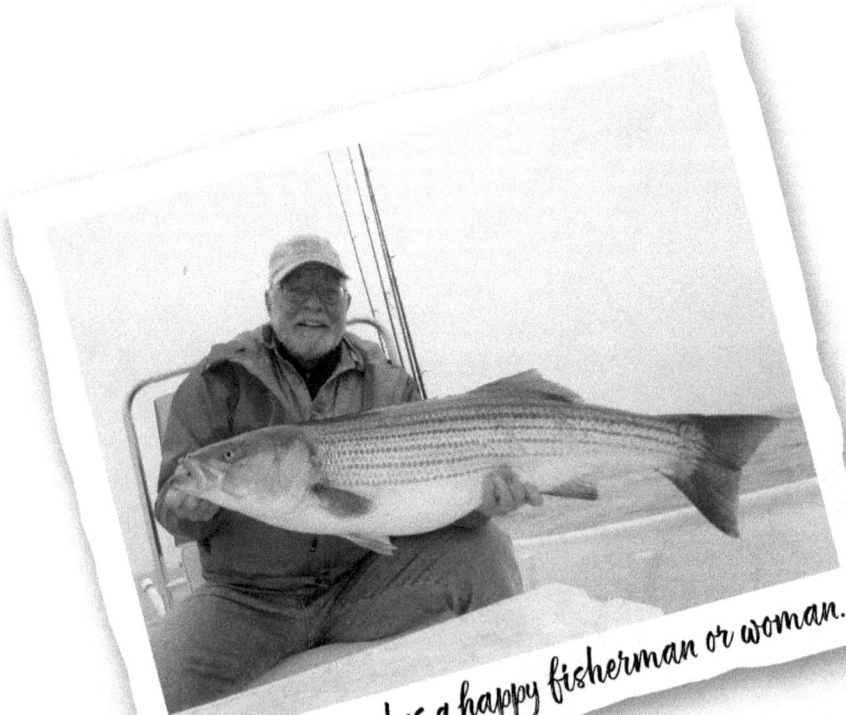

A big fish makes a happy fisherman or woman.

Pleased to Meet You

AND, ONCE AGAIN, TO MEET SPRING

Spring is here, but since I've been seduced too often into believing the end of winter was at hand, I am determined to hold back my enthusiasm. If I don't, I know it is just a matter of time before it is smashed against a spate of freezing, sullen rain and brutish, relentless wind.

Yet I know these rains and winds will flush through the marshes and wetlands. Vegetation that has died and begun to decay under the past winter's extremes will begin drifting out in the creeks and rivers just as the Bay's creatures awaken from their slumber. Silversides, Bay anchovies, grass shrimp and the mussels, clams and oysters will feast on this rich soup and grow fat again.

During the next several weeks, the shad, herring, and white perch flexing their vital muscles, will begin to spawn, just as the yellow perch have been for weeks already. This is also the time of year that larger stripers that have long ago left the Bay to become migratory fish return to the Chesapeake to spawn in their fresher natal waters. In the Maryland/Virginia waters, the Tidewaters, stripers acquire the colloquial name of rockfish because of their propensity to be found anywhere there is rocky structure. Life is bursting forth.

I was not born on the Chesapeake but on another large piece of water, Lake Erie, another kindred environment. In the mid-20th century, Lake Erie boasted the largest freshwater commercial fishery in the world and a superb recreational fishery as well. Just twenty-five years later, the lake had died from neglect and pollution. Erie today has recovered some of its past glory, but I have never returned to fish.

Chesapeake Country has been my rebirth, and I have been a grateful child. Having once lost a treasure, I value the one I have now with eyes that do not take anything for granted. Every time I cross a bridge, I bless myself on the water below. This country is rich with life, and the rivers and the creeks are her arteries, streaming nutrients and energy wherever they course. They feed the land as well as the Bay, birds and animals as well as fish and crabs. These plentiful waterways are her beauty and the source of her bounty.

I have been an avid sportsman throughout the years, much to the detriment of my professional life. Early on, I suffered through more than a few years of conflict struggle, but the outside eventually won. I kept the job, but the outdoors ruled my life.

I've gathered a few professional awards over the years in spite of my sporting obsession, but I have no idea where the plaques are. My walls at home in Cape St. Claire are covered with pictures of dogs, boats, birds, fish and friends, some in orange clothes and more in baggy shorts with rods in their hands. They all bring a smile to my face and put a lift in my step whenever I pass by. And when spring is near in Maryland, I know the next cycle of my life is also beginning.

Retired some years now, I've made some ambitious outdoor plans for the coming season. Though I'm dedicated, I have to admit that I am not the a master of any field. My luck comes late in any effort I make, but I've been blessed with a bundle of enthusiasm, and I value that highly. There are fishers, boaters and hunters who are more expert—though I doubt any enjoy it more.

In these essays, written for *Bay Weekly* newspaper from 2006 through 2019, I hope to convey some of the glories of the Chesapeake and to share my outdoor adventures and the practical knowledge I've gained along the way. I've been tromping about the tidewater for more than a half century and still have much to discover. I hope my experience draws you to Maryland's outdoors and enriches your adventures.

I'd love to share my addiction, for it's one of the few that can enrich a life endlessly.

The early-bird rockfish gang at Sandy Point State Park

The Early-Bird Rockfish Gang

DRESS WARM TO CATCH 'EM BY THE SHORE

Rockfish season is still a month away, but already a small crowd of dedicated anglers is breaking out gear. Their tackle is rather odd for the coming trophy season. They don't favor the short, stout-as-a-broomstick trolling outfits used by Bay skippers. These specialized anglers prefer equipment more common among coastal surf fishermen.

Their rods are 9- to 12-foot long with lengthy butts, and they are hung with big spinning or casting reels capable of 300 or more yards of 20-to 30-pound mono or 30-to 65-pound braid. Their terminal setups are 30-to 50-pound leaders and big circle hooks rigged with 3-to-6-ounce sinkers. Their bait of choice: bloodworms, 12 inchers, as big as they can find.

The first couple of weeks these early birds are out, fishing is catch and release only. But by the season opener, they will have sussed the tempo of the striper migration and will be ready to slide some rockfish giants into their big coolers.

Sandy Point, Fort Smallwood and Matapeake state parks as well as Anne Arundel County's Thomas Point Park are frequented by the cognoscenti. To the south, Point Lookout at the mouth of the Potomac has been drawing larger and larger numbers of anglers willing to suffer the wind, chill and rain.

This tactic, strangely enough, is relatively new. Big migratory fish surely have been cruising the shoreline looking for a snack as long as they've been returning from the ocean to spawn. Yet most anglers have traditionally pursued them by dragging big lures behind big boats on heavy tackle.

Perhaps it was the economic downturn that forced some to remain shore-bound. Perhaps the successes of a small number of dedicated fishers were finally noted. Whatever the reason, more and more anglers have been showing up in the spring to soak a big, whole bloodworm on the bottom and hope for a 40-plus incher to discover it.

When fresh menhaden become available, many anglers will switch to them. Some fanatics will even search out herring or shad that have been legally harvested elsewhere (it's prohibited to take either in any part of the Chesapeake). But the bottom line is that these guys catch fish, and often regularly.

Many anglers prefer night fishing when the big rockfish are more apt to frequent the shallows. But I have also interviewed those who maintain banker's hours, arriving about 9 a.m. and fishing through to the afternoon. Their theory is that as the majority of the fish are unpredictable, one might as well be as comfortable as possible when pursuing them. All of these guys catch fish, sometimes lots of them.

Enduring the weather is a major part of the early-spring fishing experience. Warm boots, woolen socks, wind proof, insulated coats, snug hats with ear covering, thick gloves, handwarmers and a thermos full of a hot beverage are almost a necessity, especially at night.

Many anglers fish multiple rigs. Two or more outfits increase the odds of hooking up and ensure that at least one line is available while changing baits or clearing a fouled line.

When shoreline fishing, sand spikes firmly set into the ground are surely a necessity. Casually propping your rod against a cooler risks it being dragged into deep water when a strong fish takes the bait.

A beach chair is another mark of an experienced angler. Shoreline fishing is characterized by long periods of inactivity interrupted by moments of adrenaline-soaked, fish-fighting panic. Being comfortable during the slower moments makes the wait much more tolerable.

Being near the water during early spring is a fine respite from the ravages of Maryland's holdover wintertime, an opportunity for an exciting interaction with nature and a fine excuse for an evening toddy or two later in the day.

Log Book
May 1975

flies for past year

#4 - 1/0
PLATINUM BLONDE - BROOKS
WHITE BUCKTAIL - TAIL
SILVER MYLAR - BODY
WHITE BUCKTAIL - WING

SPECIES - BONITO, LADYFISH
TROUT
(YELLOW OVER WHITE ALSO)

#10
SPONGE RUBBER SPIDER
RUBBER HACKLE
(FINNEYSPORTS TACKLE)
COLORS - BLACK OR
GREEN BODY, WHITE LEGS,
BLACK THREAD
SUPERB FOR BLUEGILLS
TIE TIGHTLY - WHIP FINISH
AND LACQUER WELL
(WARREN - KORA)

#6 - #2
UPSIDE DOWN FLY
PINK, YELLOW, OR
WHITE CHENILLE - BODY
WHITE BUCKTAIL - WING (ALSO CALFTAIL)
RED, BLACK, WHITE - HEAD
MYLAR STRIP IN
WING - OPTIONAL

SPECIES - ANYTHING IN SHALLOW
WATER

#2 - 2/0 4" LONG (NICKS)
BLUEFISH FLY -
YELLOW BLACK OR GREEN OVER
WHITE BUCKTAIL - WING
MYLAR STRIPS
BLACK OR
FLOURESCENT RED HEAD
TIED HALFWAY BACK ON
HOOK SHANK

SPECIES - ANYTHING
WITH TEETH

WEEDLESS STREAMER
TIE ON 20-30 LB test
mono with tail -
bend under and
secure at head
BASS, TROUT IN
WEEDS

WHITE BEST ALL
AROUND COLOR
FOR SALT
MYLAR HELPS
PINK & YELLOW
2ND

SMALL SIZES BETTER
FOR FEEDING FISH

LARGE SIZES FOR
BLIND CASTING
PLENTY OF MYLAR

A page from Doyle's 1975 fishing log.

How to Catch More Fish

THE SECOND-BEST WAY IS TO KEEP A LOG BOOK

The single best way to improve your odds of catching fish is to increase your time on the water. For that there is no substitute. If, however, you are looking for a plan to improve the odds of hooking up, over the long run the single most effective strategy is keeping a log book.

Human recall is not a dependable process. We tend to quickly forget the unremarkable, remembering only our more significant successes—and perhaps the occasional disaster. Everything else gets pushed aside in the avalanche of information from our technologically dense environment.

A log book aids recall immeasurably. Without one, you may be re-experiencing many things every year. In five years, instead of five seasons of cumulative fishing experience, your recall may be replaying one season's experience five times.

For my log book, I use three-by-five side-bound spiral note pads, side bound because a short pencil fits in the binding. I keep a pad with me all the time because I never know when someone is going to give me a hot tip, which I record in the log as well.

When I'm fishing, I try to write conditions down as soon as I start and results just after I quit. Some people, I'm told, are more fortunate in having the discipline to faithfully record information days later. I have never met such a person.

Vital data can vary. While on the Bay, tide, temperature, water clarity, light conditions (cloudy, bright, etc.), wind force and direction are essential as well as the location and the depth at which fish are caught. Freshwater data aren't exactly the same, but the process is analogous. The lure or bait that got them and how it was presented are always helpful.

Moon phase is helpful as well. I've found the new moon more productive than the full moon. I still fish both phases, though, because I've also noted a consistent exception: Overcast conditions during the full moon can be especially good. That insight came straight out of my logs.

The circumstances of trips where you don't catch anything can be valuable, too. Keeping in mind the eternal axiom the best time to go fishing is whenever you can, the information from unsuccessful trips may help you modify your techniques to adapt to adverse conditions—or at least to lower your expectations under certain familiar circumstances.

Review your entries from time to time, particularly at the end of one year and the beginning of the next. Look for trends, patterns and coincidences. On a day-to-day basis, it is easy to overlook a relationship between weather, tide, temperature or other specific circumstances and fishing success.

So when a dry spell comes along, I can look back at earlier years when Bay salinity was high because of low rainfall. Once upon a spring, salinity paralleled a run of big stripers. Oversize croakers, big perch and spot were unusually plentiful. Summer was followed by an exceptional fall run of sea trout, and the rockfish moved early up into the tributaries, providing exceptional shallow-water striper fishing in September and October. Without my log book, I'd never have remembered all those specifics.

Another byproduct of log keeping is that it makes you more observant. The angler who may initially attribute a successful fishing trip to superior skill may on reflection replace that assumption. It's not, after all, about us. It's about the fish. Since their behavior can be in flux, responding to the constant flow of the external environment, it's helpful to review the circumstances that invoke the actions. Fortune favors the aware.

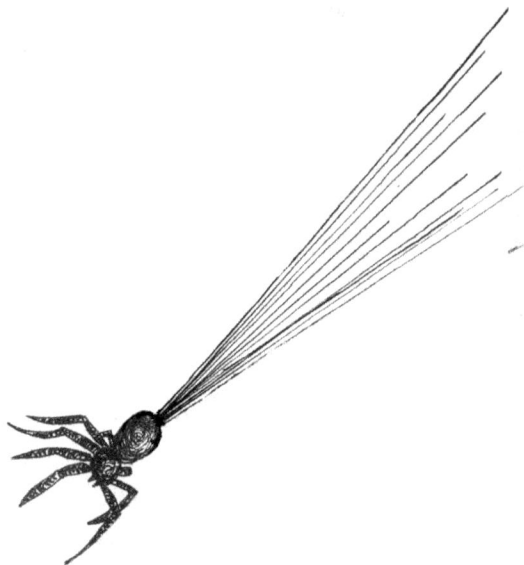

Airborne Arachnids

Drifting high across most landscapes this time of year, sometimes to altitudes of 16,000 feet or more, are airborne travelers that few people notice, though the fliers may number in the thousands.

They are spiders seeking new territories.

These ballooning or sailing spiders are generally the smaller of the many spider varieties and are borne aloft by winds on gossamer filaments spun by the spider, forming a pyramid canopy that can carry them for sometimes thousands of miles.

A migratory activity, especially for young hatchlings, sailing or ballooning is a natural mode of transportation that disburses the spiders from their nesting or home site. When they are ready to travel, the spiders instinctually climb high in the trees or onto higher terrain and spin their webbing. Then, standing on tiptoes, they wait for the wind to bear them away.

Because of their size, they are difficult to see, but you can sometimes spot them on a sunny day by looking up for their long, silvery threads. On a recent fishing trip on the Chesapeake, we were rewarded by spotting a dozen or so of the travelers, a few of which found refuge on our skiff, disappearing into the nooks and crevices as soon as they landed.

Aerial arachnids that come down on the Bay are not doomed, as they are so light that, with their naturally water-repellent feet, they can skate or scamper across the water's surface, often to great distance, eventually reaching more hospitable territory. Or nature's airborne rangers can spin new webs and wait to be carried aloft again.

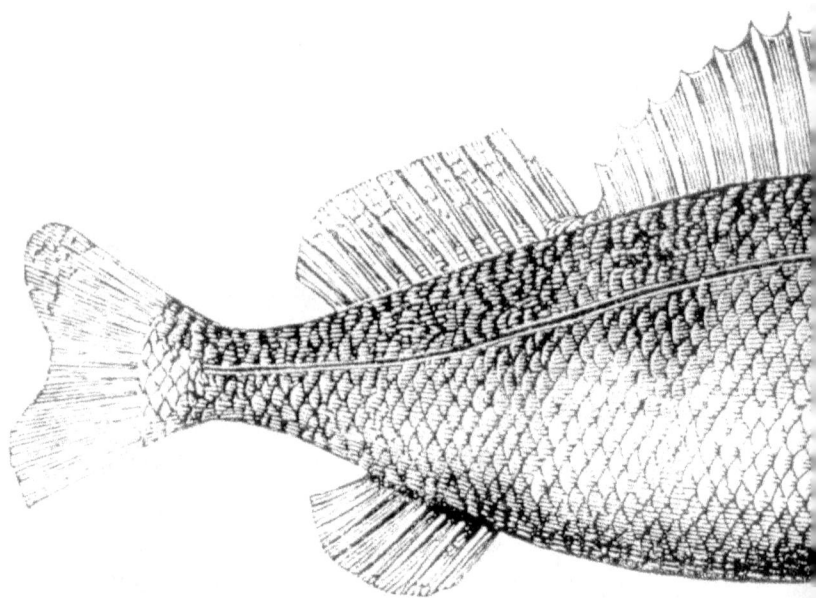

April

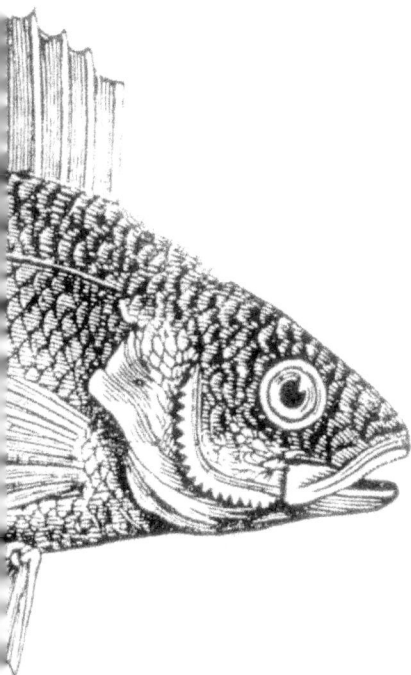

A most generous fish, the white perch is the Bay's most abundant catch.

The Day Was All Wrong, Except for Morone Americana

WE FOUND A SILVER LINING IN WHITE PERCH THIS CLOUDY DAY

The fishing trip started up late. Because of work, Mike Eberberger and I couldn't leave until three in the afternoon. Then forgotten items further botched our departure, until we didn't even get on the road until four.

Once we got on the Choptank, we'd be facing the brisk, windy weather of earliest spring. All together, we held out little hope for a successful trip. But this season, we had decided that we would go whenever we could, no planning for the perfect conditions with plenty of leisure, no cherry picking the 10-day weather forecast. We were going to fish every chance we got.

Hours earlier, we had hoped to cash in on the yellow perch run. But at this point we would have been happy with anything.

As we hastily launched my small skiff at a northern Choptank ramp at about 4:45 p.m., prospects looked even gloomier, and not just because it was a windy, cloudy day with sunset hardly more than an hour away. The water was also exceedingly low, not an optimum condition for finding active fish.

Switching to an exploratory frame of mind, we decided that if we weren't apt to find fish, it was a good day to check out the stream bank and bottom structure, because with the low water we sure could see plenty of that.

Heading downstream, we paused from time to time to cast to the occasional fishy-looking cove or fallen tree. For the most part, we were just looking, noting promising areas for future trips. For the longest time, the only action was retrieving our lures from overhanging branches and underwater snags.

Then, in a particularly nondescript stretch of river that was unique only in that it had virtually no apparent fish-holding structure, Mike made a random cast and hooked up with a nice white perch.

That was surprising, first because it was early in the year for them. Whites usually don't start running until later in March. Second, there seemed to be no reason for fish to be holding on that particular section of the water. We were using medium-sized mummichogs or mud minnows, lip hooked off a one-ounce sinker.

I kept the boat steady in the current with the electric motor while Mike unhooked the chunky devil, rebaited and cast again to that spot, if only to confirm the 10-inch fish was just a wandering stray.

He immediately hooked up again. Fighting the apparently sizeable fish with one hand, he groped with his other for our bow anchor, found it and lowered it over the side. I shut down the motor and reached for my rod. This, apparently, was a rare springtime honey hole.

THE BAY'S MOST ABUNDANT CATCH

Morone Americana will hardly ever pass up a bait or a battle. Their favorite live baits are grass shrimp, bloodworms, minnows, clam snouts and peeler and soft crab, but just sometimes they're just as happy to bite on artificial lures. Spinner baits such as

Super Rooster Tails, Beetle Spins and Mepps can be reliable producers, and the smaller versions of swimming plugs such as Rat-L-Traps and Shad Raps often seduce lunker whites.

Devotees swear by small silver or gold spoons, and others by the many mini-sized soft plastics of the Bass Assassin, the Fin-S and the Berkley Gulp! series. Whatever method or device you choose to pursue these sporty devils, you won't lack for action.

The most populous fish in the Bay, white perch spend their whole lives within the confines of Chesapeake waters. A close cousin of the striped bass, the fish has an olive back, silvery white sides with one distinctive lateral stripe and sharp, dorsal, pectoral and anal fins. Use care in handling them or you will get stuck.

The fish can grow slowly, the females taking three years to sexually mature and probably five years to get to 9 inches, a reasonably edible size. A 12-incher is a whopper. When they spawn, as they are now doing, they can spew out up to 150,000 eggs in efforts that last over three weeks. The eggs hatch in one to six days. Congregating in the headwaters of virtually all the Bay tributaries, they will continue to spawn off and on until late May.

Incredible fecund, they are remarkable resilient to the pressures that our relentless population growth has brought upon them. Numerically, Morone Americana is the most harvested finfish in the Chesapeake, both commercially and recreationally.

An estuarine creature with large populations in New York's Hudson Bay as well as the Chesapeake, the white perch spawns in fresh water but prefers more brackish water the rest of the year. It is rarely found in salt water, though it has an established population in some of Maryland's fresh water reservoirs especially Liberty, Loch Raven and Prettyboy.

Strangely, for a fish with such an ardent following, it has few aliases. The bigger perch are sometimes called black backs for the darker colors they assume when they get older and larger, but otherwise they are simply referred to as white perch or just plain perch.

CATCHING 'EM

For the next hour of that late March afternoon, silver flashed everywhere in the surrounding water as we battled white perch after white perch from that otherwise unremarkable 15-yard section. On virtually every cast, we got hook-ups. We were frequently fighting fish simultaneously.

There were certainly a fair number of smaller fish, but there were also a whole lot of table-sized whites, many over 10 inches and a few just short of 12. Those above 9 1/2 inches went into the fish box; the shorts back over the side. Our arms ached from the constant battle. No matter what their size, these early fish were full of scrap.

One more welcome surprise: Most of these fish, especially the bigger ones were empty of roe. Even at this early date, they had already completed the spawn. I relish the occasional treat of fried perch roe, but I prefer to let the big, egg-laden females go on their way to procreate.

Before the sun had descended the horizon, we had run out of minnows and had a box full of handsome white perch. Wrists sore and weary, we headed home. Already planning a fish fry the next day, we congratulated ourselves. We had discovered a silvery lining in an seemingly gray day.

Old Town Discovery canoe,
perfect for shallow-water fishing.

The New Canoe

WITH ONE WIFE, ONE DOG AND FIVE BOATS, I'M A LUCKY MAN

My maiden voyage with my latest acquisition did not unfold without problems. It had been a dozen years at least since I had last paddled a canoe, so I hadn't planned on doing much the first time out other than reacquainting myself with the basics.

I had brought along a light spin rod, but didn't have high hopes for catching. The white perch run had been over for a while, though I suspected one or two might be among any upriver stragglers.

It was a beautiful, early morning, and a warm sun had dissipated the previous evening's chill. Crew on the outing was my first mate, Sophie, a German shorthair who would go just about anywhere with me without complaint.

Setting the light and elegant 14-foot canoe at the edge of the water, I packed in my paddle, the rod, a small life preserver and tackle bag. Sophie settled herself amidships, I took my seat and confidently pushed us off from the beach.

All went well for the first 75 feet, at which time our craft cleared the first point of land, exposing us to a brisk upriver breeze. The canoe's bow, sitting high because of the way I had loaded the boat, caught the wind and swang smartly around just as Sophie, detecting the scent of something interesting in the freshened air, lurched to the side for a better sniff. Uhh–ohhh!

Luckily, the canoe had great secondary stability. The unexpected heel and change in direction had caused me only a brief instant of panic. But the thought of capsizing, less than a minute from launch, brought on a flush of embarrassment.

I attempted to casually J-stroke the canoe back on course, but it didn't work. The new wind frustrated my every move.

Finally abandoning the effort as futile, I took the new craft back to the beach. Adjustments were in order. I moved Sophie farther forward, rearranged my tackle and gear away from under foot and tried again.

This time, with the bow lower and no longer a wind sail, my foot position unencumbered and paddling leverage improved, we made much better progress. The narrower beam up forward also limited Sophie's movements, so my first mate could lean and sniff to her heart's content without upsetting our stability. I relaxed and resumed relearning my paddle strokes.

SEEK AND YOU SHALL FIND

Obtaining this noble craft was not a planned event. It happened on an impulse, prompted by some recent surgery. Doctor's orders forbade me any form of strenuous lifting or physical activity for eight weeks. That had resulted in far too many shore-bound days. Life was not good for me and didn't look to get better any time soon.

Then one afternoon, as I was whiling away my down time by investigating the boats for sale section of Craigslist, inspiration struck me. Overnight, and for a modest sum, I assumed ownership of a used light weight and handsome 14-foot Old Town canoe in dark green.

My wife, God bless her, tried to ignore the sudden presence among the other four boats that cluttered our yard while

I assured her that I intended to promptly move the new acquisition to a spot on our community's dinghy rack.

Furthermore, the light weight would not violate my doctor's prohibition on lifting heavy objects. I would merely be dragging the craft a short distance to the water, not lifting it. And paddling, I added, would hardly prove strenuous along our sheltered coves.

I was pleased the first day out as Sophie and I cruised easily along while I cast, uneventfully as it turned out, to likely looking piers and points and observed the local wildlife. Though I caught as little as I had expected, other thoughts began to form in my head as we moved along.

While the canoe was obviously perfect for shallow-water fishing for perch and pickerel, the craft should, I thought also prove ideal for some light crabbing. I had long ago perfected a standard operation for trotlining, but it took lot of effort and preparation and my powered skiff. That was great for securing a bushel or more of crabs. But if I wanted only a dozen or so, the trotline was overkill.

Crabbing with a canoe and four or five hand lines baited with chicken necks would take virtually no prep at all. I could be on the water within 15 minutes of the decision to go. The easily maneuverable canoe would also be ideal for stealthily visiting the numerous nearby pilings and piers for some quiet morning crab-dipping with a small, long-handled net.

I no longer felt handicapped by my recent infirmity as I realized I was discovering new and a much simpler opportunity. When one door closes, do not despair, for others usually open. That maxim was precisely true for me and my new canoe.

Five steps of knot tying:

1. Put the line through the eye of the hook

2. Wrap the short end of the line around the long part five times.

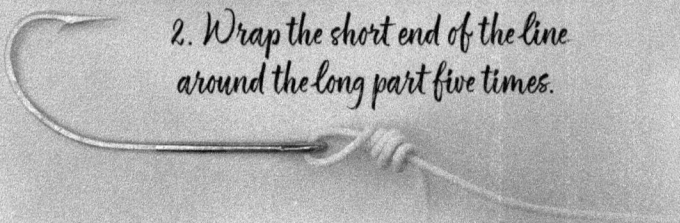

3. Put the short end through the first loop, closest to the hook.

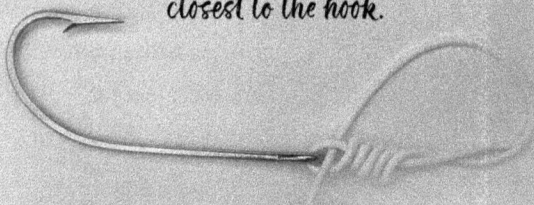

4. Put the short end through the large loop at the end of the wrapped section.

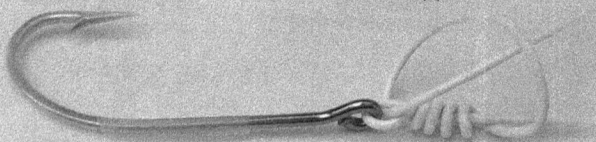

5. Moisten the knot with saliva. Then pull tight.

Knotty Matters

WHAT KNOTS TO KNOW

One single critical thing an angler can do to help catch more big fish is learn to tie the right knot correctly. In a life of fishing and after working in an area sports store for a good number of years and listening to countless tales of big fish broken off and inexplicable separations, I've learned many anglers aren't sure which knot to tie or how to tie it.

The weakest link in the connection between fish and fisherman is the knot. Common household and sailing knots such as the bowline, square knot, granny knot, overhand knot and the various cleat hitches and the like make poor bends for fishing applications. Generally these fastenings will seriously reduce the breaking strength of fishing lines or not hold at all, slipping out when extreme pressure is applied. Do not use them.

Referring to books, magazines and web sites devoted to knot tying is a quick route to information overload. There are so many knots described, they are all so different and the appropriate application descriptions rudimentary: Who can tell exactly which need to be mastered? It would be impossible to master them all. What's worse, many of these sources contain one serious piece of misinformation.

Years ago when fishing line was made from twisted heavy cotton and then Dacron, the most popular fishing knot used was the clinch knot. Tying this knot involves putting the line through the eye of the hook or lure, wrapping the tag (short) end of the line around the standing line six or seven times, then putting the tag end back through the loop formed at the hook eye and pulling the whole affair tight.

The clinch was a good knot.

But if you're using modern fishing lines—nylon monofilaments, co-filaments, fluorocarbons and especially the newer braided lines—the clinch knot under stress will promptly and invariably fail. The knot is not designed to allow for line stretch.

THE CAN'T-DO-WITHOUT KNOT

The one basic knot for general angling applications is the improved clinch knot.

The improved clinch—also known as a fisherman's knot or a lucky seven—is based on the clinch knot, adding one critical step: After the tag end is pulled through the loop at the hook eye, it must also be passed through the last loop made, then moistened with saliva and pulled tight.

If the knot is not moistened or otherwise lubricated, it will be difficult to completely tighten, an important element in knot strength. It is also quite possible to severely reduce the line integrity by generating excessive heat at the knot site due to the unlubricated line friction.

An improved clinch knot thus tied will test at close to 100 percent of any line's breaking strength and will not slip. If you know how to tie only this one knot, you will get through an average day of fishing in fine shape.

Do note, however, if you're using the newer ultra-thin braided line, because of its tendency to cut into itself or slip, you will need to double up the line before tying the improved clinch (or any fishing knot).

Practice tying this knot until you can do it without thinking. All knots should be moistened with saliva and tightened gradually and forcefully until they are completely tight.

MORE HELPFUL KNOTS

Still, a person can't help noticing countless interesting knots in the literature. Five or six more can be useful to the average angler.

At the risk of oversimplification (and noting that blue-water and extreme light-tackle anglers use additional knot variations that can be quite complex) these are the Palomar knot, the barrel knot, the blood knot, the surgeon's loop, the uni-knot (including its variation the double-uni) and the Albright knot. Fly anglers, because of the uniqueness of their main lines and leaders, must add the nail and surgeon's knots to this list.

Angling-oriented knot-tying books that feature these knots are: *Practical Fishing Knots* by Lefty Kreh; *Waterproof Book of Knots: Sport Fishing* by Geoff Wilson; and *The Complete Book of Fishing Knots* by Geoffrey Budworth. Numerous animated tying instructions for all of these knots and more can be found online by typing animated fishing knots.

Only after mastering the improved clinch knot should you progress to learning others. I suggest the Palomar next. It is one of the strongest and easier-to-tie connections, but its application is limited. The shortcoming will become obvious as you learn to tie it.

The next in importance is the barrel knot for tying two sections of line together, the leader to the main line, for example. Master each new knot before tackling another and continually practice them.

Whatever knot you're using, always moisten the line with saliva (for lubrication) when pulling it tight. Otherwise heat from the friction of the knot tightening will weaken the line.

One last and very important recommendation: When you have tied your knot, always examine it closely one last time. If it doesn't look exactly right, cut it off and tie it again. You will never regret it.

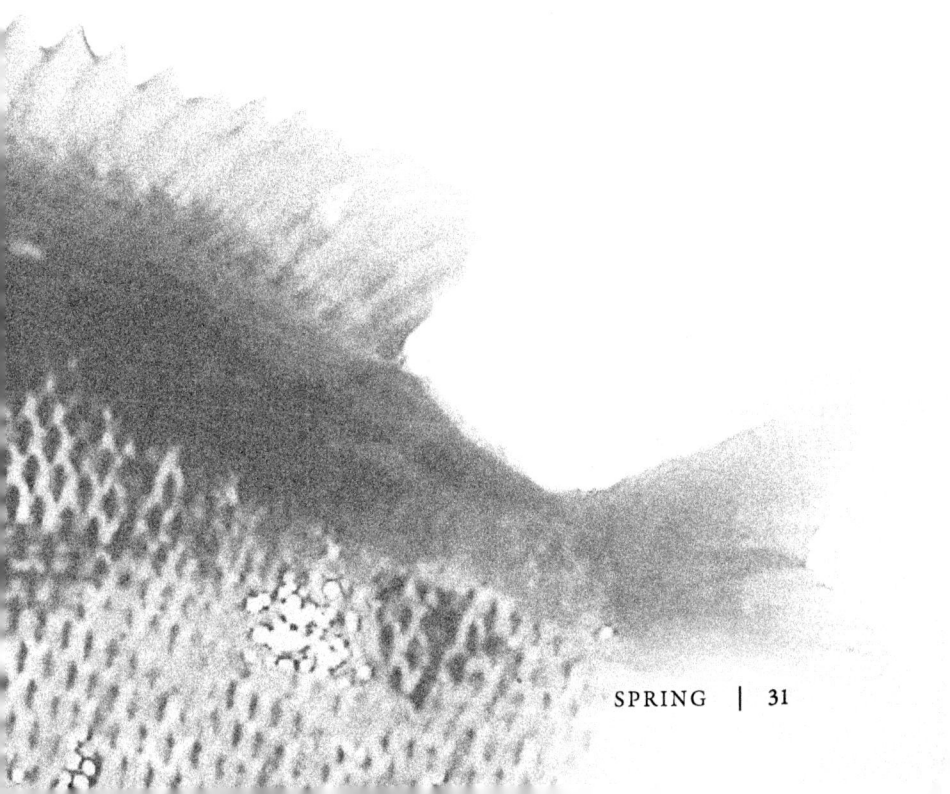

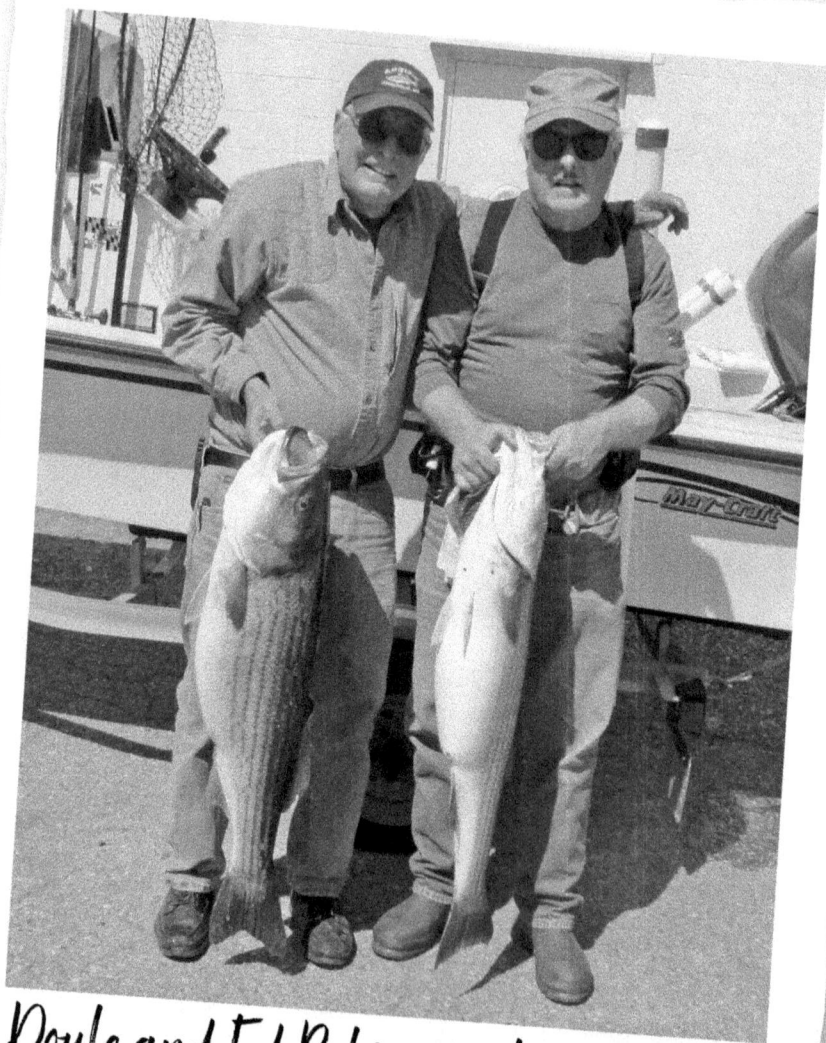

Doyle and Ed Robinson show off their trophy rockfish caught in Doyle's skiff.

Fishing Light Tackle for Trophy Rockfish

FIND 'EM, CHUM 'EM, PRAY FOR GOOD LUCK

When the reel spool began turning under my thumb, I knew it was no ordinary rockfish on the end of my line; this one seemed extra determined. Counting to seven, I threw the Abu 5600 reel into gear, and when the line came tight, set the hook. Then my rod bent over to the corks and a stiffly set drag howled as the fish really hit the gas. This one had to be trophy sized. If only I could get it to the boat.

We were anchored up south of the Hackett's can buoy at the mouth of the Severn River in 35 feet of water on a morning that was glassy calm despite a small-craft warning from NOAA the day before. Not deterred, my fishing companion Ed Robinson checked another forecast, which predicted light winds until almost noon.

We agreed that if the winds were calm, we would head out and fish until the weather turned. Launching my 17-foot skiff, we were on station by 8 a.m. A half-hour later, our four rods were rigged and baited with large chunks of fresh menhaden. A chum bag over the stern was spewing small bits of ground fish into the falling tidal current as we guessed that we had only about three hours of ebb left before slack water.

Then Ed had a run and landed a fat and healthy 23-incher, a good sign there were fish around. We quickly released it. Then, a few minutes later, my bruiser hit.

SPRING | 33

Chumming during trophy rockfish season is a long-odds affair. Because the big fish are spawning and moving alone, erratically, and in small packs, it is impossible to determine patterns. They don't stay in one place for very long, so catching reports are mostly useless. Locating legal fish is pretty much a matter of luck.

In years when a larger minimum size has been set by the Atlantic States Marine Fisheries Commission, it may be even more difficult to find keepers when fishing bait.

Trolling is the most reliably productive technique during trophy season as you're covering far more water and using big lures that exclude the smaller guys. But if you want to use light tackle for a trophy size, you've got to fish bait.

Our four outfits were medium-heavy, 6½-foot casting rods with Abu 5600 casting reels loaded with fresh 150 yards of 20-pound fluoro-coated mono, with fish finder rigs, 2-ounce sinkers and stout 9/0 hooks on 24-inch 30-pound fluoro leaders.

REELING IN A RUNAWAY TRAIN

It was 20 minutes into the battle before I got a glimpse of the striper. It was definitely a good one. Calming myself and making sure not to force things, I eased it to the side of the boat. Ed got most of the fish into the meager net. It took both of us to lift it over the gunnel. The lunker's big tail ran well past the deck-mounted 36-inch measuring tape, so we were sure it was legal. After a quick picture we eased the handsome giant into my fish box and iced it down.

Ed had pulled all of our rigs out of the water during the battle to avoid tangles, so it took another 20 minutes to get them cleared, baited and back in the water. After that we didn't have long to wait.

One of Ed's rigs twitched, then the clicker on the reel started screaming as the fish picked up the bait and headed away at speed. It was another runaway train.

The fight mirrored my own. Almost a twin of the first one, this burly rascal also hung half out of my net as we barely managed it up over the side. Two giants inside of half an hour.

Done by 10 a.m. with two trophies in the box, their tails sticking out a the lid bulging open, we headed for the ramp grinning like fools. An hour later, a stiff north wind pushed three-foot seas with shore-to-shore whitecaps.

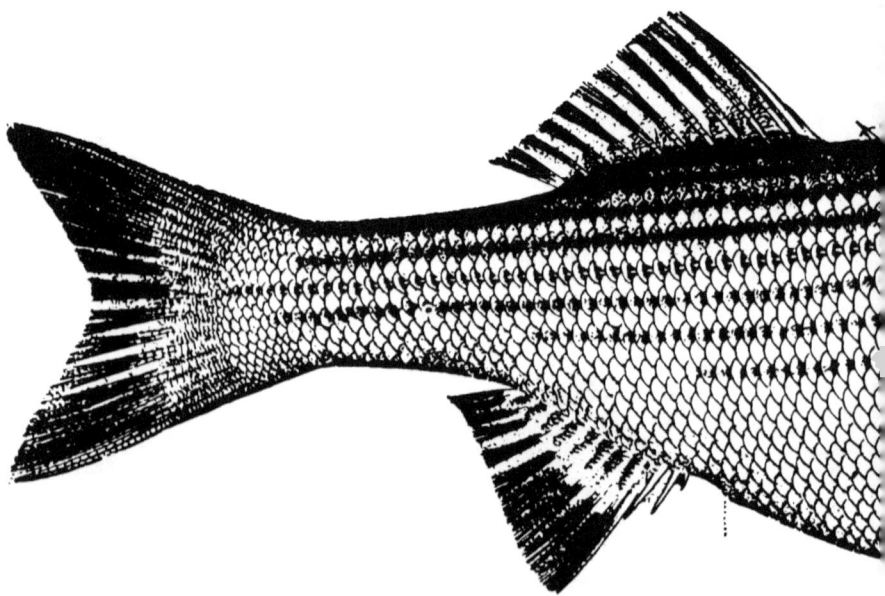

May

Doyle hooked this fat bluegill on his fly rod.

Torn Between Two Loves

SALT AND SWEET WATER EACH HAVE MY HEART

This time of year brings conflict for me. The trophy rockfish season beckoning with the promise of big fish is a temptation almost impossible to resist.

Yet there is another of nature's sirens murmuring in my ear. This one promises even more delicious treats to be had as the sweetwater bite blossoms—

A smashing surface strike throws foam water everywhere, and the fish's momentum carries it up and out, giving me a brief glimpse of a colorful profile, thick and powerful. Setting the hook firmly, I try to keep the fish away from the tangle of lily pads from which it launched its attack. I can feel violent headshakes as it turns its broad body sideways and exerts a pressure that bends my slim rod down to the cork handle. I fear it is too much stress, but I know if the fish reaches the roots of those pads, I will lose it for sure. Then, just as quickly, it is gone.

My heart hammers as I retrieve my ravaged popper. The thin wire hook is bent open. I have lost a trophy. The bluegill probably weighs almost a pound.

Each spring as the trees bud, the daffodils burst into bloom and shoots of grass start to weave their luscious green carpet over winter's barren leavings, in the sweetwater, bluegill, largemouth bass, crappie, pickerel and perch emerge from their deep-winter lairs.

Answering nature's call, they are swarming to shallow, shoreline locations, scouting out spawning sites and performing their intricate and secret dances to attract mates. They will attract anglers as well.

This is the time of year when you can quietly slip a canoe or small skiff off the banks of a wooded shoreline and cast a spinner, bug or fly to tempting pockets of water with explosive results. Though the fish are of modest size compared to their saltier cousins, they do not lack for aggressiveness or dramatics.

There is no more theatrical image than that of a gill-rattling, head-shaking, five-pound largemouth launching itself into the air to protest an angler's deception. And for fierce aggressiveness, few compare to a bluegill's willingness to smash a small, floating bug that has had the impertinence to invade its domain.

The crappie *pronounced with a broad 'ah' sound* are gathered along deeper shorelines, but they are schooling and preparing to mate as well. These brilliant green, speckled beauties provide a singular challenge. Hard fighters eager to take a small minnow, spinner bait or wet fly, crappie demand a delicate hand. With a large but fragile mouth structure that has earned them the alias papermouth, they can shed a fishhook easier than a tabby cat its winter coat. And their table quality is such that few anglers choose to share any information as to their whereabouts.

Then there is the deadly U-Boat of the freshwater, the pickerel. Silently lurking in ambush behind screens of brush, downed tree limbs or just-emerging weed lines, these long, toothy, water wolves are murder incorporated. Their attack is sudden and fierce, and if you're lucky enough to hook up with a big one, you'll have a spectacular battle on your hands.

All this as the sweetwater countryside awakens from winter. Turtles of all sizes and types arise from their hibernation beds in the bottom muck to ascend shorelines and even the branches of downed trees to catch the new warmth of our spring sun.

Brilliant royal-blue kingfishers swoop shorelines to catch small, unsuspecting fish. The throaty frogs are busy sending their songs across the emerging lily pads to prospective mates.

Herons and egrets in beautiful climax plumage stalk the shorelines, home from their winter migrations to far-distant southern climes. Across the water, the calls of geese and ducks—even the eerie cries of a few loons that have decided Maryland is far enough north for them—echo as they establish the boundaries of their newly chosen nesting sites.

The open water of the mighty Chesapeake does beckon strongly this time of year. But Maryland's outdoor temptations are many and varied. After our long and miserable winter, that's just what we all need.

Lowrance fish finder

Don't Fish Blind to What's Below

MASTERING YOUR ELECTRONICS
WILL INCREASE YOUR CATCH

I've had a great past two weeks fishing the Chesapeake during this early spring season. Nice rockfish to 34 inches were in multiple small mobs, hanging in 20 to 30 feet of water. When I located one on the finder, they promptly attacked any jigs or baits we dropped on them. A number of friends had the same experience.

Yet later this week, I heard from anglers who had cruised the same waters and hadn't been able to catch anything. What's more, they told me, they generally had trouble catching rockfish, despite serious effort.

Digging deeper I ferreted out a common denominator. All had electronic fish finders on their craft but weren't up to speed on using them. Depth was about all they understood.

It's a dictum of fishing the salt that 90 percent of the task is locating the fish. The single most effective tool in finding fish on large bodies of water, like the Chesapeake, is the electronic fish finder.

Locating fish with the finder does not guarantee that you will catch them. But it is impossible to catch fish that aren't there, no matter how hard you try.

The electronic fish finder is the most revolutionary tool available to anglers. It's a tool with a story that dates back to the sinking of the *Titanic*. The part of the iceberg hit by the cruise ship was underwater and unobservable to the navigating crew.

After the disaster, work immediately began on how to detect below-surface objects. First developed was an echo-range apparatus, an early form of sonar, based on the navigational methods of dolphins. Canadian Reginald Fessenden's invention was used in World War I to help Allied ships find submarines.

Today's fish finders are able instruments with multiple options to tailor them to your unique marine environment and detect just about anything underwater you'd care to find. Based to a certain extent on anti-submarine technology, these babies are so technically sophisticated that they remain illegal for export to foreign countries.

But a few days ago I was reminded of just how daunting dealing with these instruments can be. My unit hiccuped during booting and failed to load. When I turned it off and back on again to reboot, I saw that most of my settings had been lost and the unit's displays were unrecognizable.

TROUBLESHOOTING THE TECHNOLOGY

It had been years since I set the machine up and fine-tuned it, so I had no memory of how I did it. With multiple screen menus each with many options, I had to go back to the manual and start over.

Turning on my unit with my boat on its trailer beside my house, I had no distractions. (Do not attempt to set up or review your settings while fishing; there is just too much going on.) With the manual in my lap, I went through setup again.

A basic menu option on any recently manufactured unit is a reset to original manufacturer defaults. That's where I started. If you are unfamiliar or uncomfortable with electronics, I recommend you begin there as well. There is little intuitive about setting up a fish finder, but most manuals are fairly helpful. If the original manual for your machine cannot be located, most manufacturers offer them on their websites. As a last resort, you can call the manufacturer and order a copy.

Once you've entered your initial settings, take a short cruise (with the manual and without your tackle) to fine-tune them. Repeat, trying different options and watching your screen to observe the effects. If your choices end in confusion, reset to the default settings and start over.

IF AT FIRST

If you remain flummoxed, there is a another solution. Almost all retailers of such units have at least one employee expert in their setup and use. In talking to a number of them, I have found them all eager to help, especially during the slow times of winter.

Disconnect the unit from the boat and take it to the store. There the technician can hook it up in-house and go over the settings, explain the options and suggest changes for your type of fishing.

There also may be software upgrades available from the manufacturer. These are generally free and can be downloaded pretty easily.

Call ahead to make sure a technician will be on hand and that they service your brand. You can also discuss aftermarket productions, such as navigational map overlays.

A well-tuned instrument will become a customized tool that meets your requirements, eye and angling techniques. The reward will come in terms of more fish in the boat and more confidence in your approach.

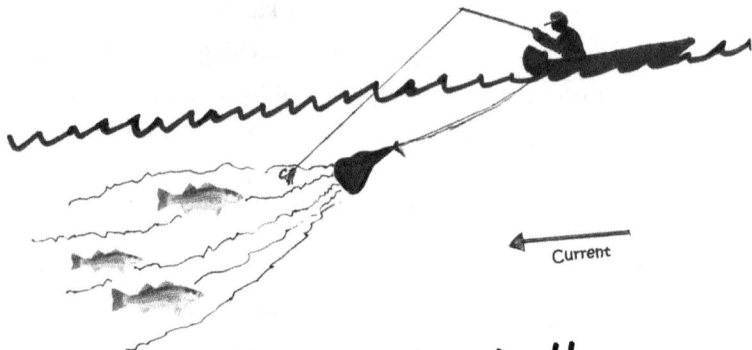

Fish respond ideally
to the perfect chumming set up.

Chumming for Summer Rockfish

TIPS ON CHUM, TACKLE AND TIDE

During the coming summer months, chumming will be one of the easiest and most effective techniques for getting a limit of rockfish in your cooler.

Chumming is essentially putting a stream of small bits of ground up baitfish into the tidal current flowing out behind an anchored boat. The smell and taste of the fish trails out and sinks down, attracting game fish, hopefully stripers, to your boat. As they seek out the source of the attractant, they will also find your hook baited with a larger chunk of the same baitfish.

Menhaden (also known as alewife, bunker or pogey) is the primary chum of choice throughout the Bay as it is a major natural food source for rockfish. They are well acquainted with both its odor and taste. Occasionally, however, anglers successfully use cat food, synthetic dry chum and the ground-up debris from a crab feast.

Generally, though, a frozen bucket of menhaden chum, suspended behind the boat in a mesh bag, is the simplest way to get the job done. When tidal currents are swift, weight the chum bag and hang it deeper so that the fish are drawn in close enough to your baits. When the current is slower, hanging the chum just off the stern will work fine.

Anglers seeking more effective approaches to the technique (usually charter boat skippers) may insist upon using only fresh-caught menhaden and grinding it onsite aboard their boat before dribbling it overboard. This superior approach will almost always result in a better, quicker bite. Still, under most circumstances, commercially frozen chum dispersed from a mesh bag will eventually get the job done.

Tackle is typically medium-heavy action spin- or bait-casting rod with lines ranging anywhere from 30-pound braid to 15-pound mono and fluorocarbon. Early in the season, all of these line choices have a reasonably good chance of success. As the summer wears on and fish wise up, most anglers will find more stripers seduced by the lighter tests of mono and fluoro.

Analyzing tide, tidal current and wind can also be essential to success. Choosing sites and times that provide a general sameness of tidal current and wind direction is critical. If the wind and tide current are opposite, your boat will be blown one way and your chum slick and baits will be carried in another direction, making very difficult conditions.

Timing of the tidal change is also important. Schools of rockfish often begin feeding at specific periods, usually sometime during the first or last two hours of tidal current. For the best chance of success, try to fish an entire six-hour tide cycle, from slack tide to slack tide.

When reading a tide chart, note that the current will not immediately reverse at the specific time and place a tide is noted. Generally, it takes about two hours after the time noted for an incoming current to slacken, then eventually begin to move out. The same is true for the low-tide cycle.

Keeping all of these variables in mind when choosing when and where to chum will save you a lot of time, allow you to concentrate on conditions that favor you the most and ultimately result in more fish in your cooler.

Tom Schneider caught two rockfish on delectable soft-crab baits.

Softshell Crab Is Gourmet Bait

BUT IT DOESN'T GUARANTEE YOU'LL CATCH A ROCKFISH

The tide was just slacking, perfect for the type of fishing I planned, as little weight was necessary to get softshell crab baits down deep where the fish were holding.

Rockfish think as highly of this delicacy, the soft phase of the Atlantic blue crab, as we do. A blue crab enters its soft phase by molting or shedding its hard shell. That's how it grows, gaining about an additional third of its previous size by ingesting water and swelling. The crab's new shell hardens within six hours. If the crab is removed from the water, however, the hardening process is interrupted. That's how we get to eat them when they are in that most delicious phase.

Some moisture is essential to keep the crab alive and fresh. But eventually, despite the best efforts of the seafood processors, the shell will begin to harden. The first stage of that hardening is the papershell stage. While the papershell is still fairly delicate (like paper), it's already become tough enough to make for poor dining.

But for rockfish—indeed any predator swimming in the Chesapeake—paper crab is still filet mignon, plus it is just firm enough to easily retain a hook. I ran the point of a 5/0 J hook through the leg joints where they meet the crab's body to provide the most secure attachment The stripers that leapt to my bait were, unfortunately, not amateurs. Grabbing an edge of the bait, they would jet off with a chunk. I would strike mightily to no apparent effect except separating the crab into smaller bits, most without a hook inside.

That how I learned the day's first lesson. The papershells were quite large. In my eagerness to tempt a really big rockfish, I had decided to go with a generous half crab. Going to smaller crab chunks without legs and claws made the baits much more effective in getting a hookup. So did a No. 2 treble hook, as the extra points keep the piece of bait together longer than a simple J hook. Note that when using natural bait, the current regulation specifies non-offset circle hooks or J hooks with a gap of less than half and inch. It is always a good idea to check with Department of Natural Resources on the regulations, as they change annually: www.eregulations.com/maryland/fishing/striped-bass

Adding a small rubber band also holds the bait more securely, as does covering the bait with a small piece of sheer mesh fabric.

Even with my bait secured, that day on the Bay had other lessons to teach me. I'm generally a firm believer in letting a hooked rockfish run. My philosophy has always been that they should be given their head. Sooner or later (usually sooner) the fish will tire, and you can gradually bring it under control and into the net.

That's what I was doing—line peeling off the reel, howling against a firmly set drag—when my fish angled the line across a nearby barnacled pier and cut me off. My usual technique is not at all wise if there is significant structure or sunken debris nearby to foul or cut your line. This location had plenty of that, and I soon lost a number of rigs to fish diving into the debris on the bottom or wrapping the line across the rough concrete bridge supports.

Soon, running low on bait, spare hooks and leaders, I cranked my drag down to near maximum. It had become all too obvious that if I didn't stop the fish and get them under control immediately on hookup, I wasn't going to land them.

Making those adjustments eventually landed the first two fish, 22- and-23-inchers. Despite tactical changes and improved hookup rates, I continued to lose many of the bigger fish fights. A few of the brutes were so powerful that my light tackle couldn't stop them before they'd somehow cut themselves loose or broke the tortured line.

Later, our line would include heavier weight leaders and running lines. Eventually I would resort to employing 50-pound braid in my running lines and short 30-pound fluoro leaders around bridge structures during early seasons when larger fish were frequently encountered.

Good luck on the Bay is not a sure thing, even with the tastiest bait. But a day on the Bay is always an adventure.

Summer

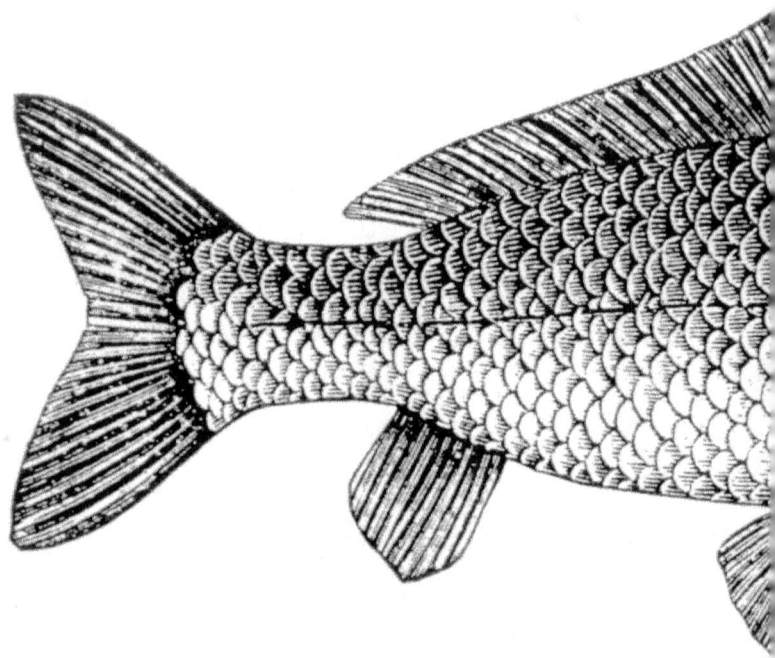

June

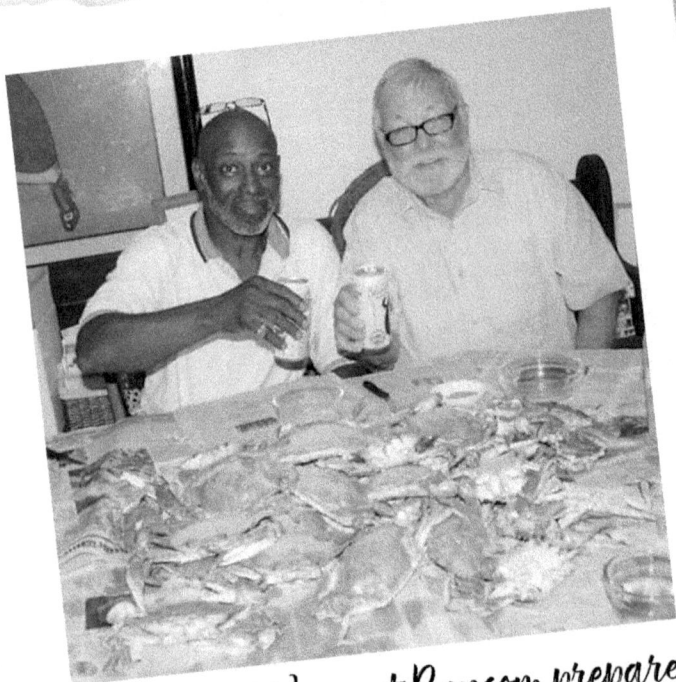

Doyle and Vincent Ransom prepare to enjoy Maryland's finest meal.

Maryland's Finest Meal

CALLINECTES SAPIDUS ARE A DELICACY
YOU CAN BRING HOME YOURSELF

The trotline came up slowly over our roller as my electric trolling motor ghosted the skiff along. A bright sun was already getting a firm grip on the morning and reminding us of a hotter day ahead.

One by one, we managed an even dozen fat jimmies that didn't even need to be measured—even with Vincent Ransom, my friend from New Jersey, manning a trotline net for his first time ever. After that, crabs kept flying out of his net and into our basket.

Within an hour and a half, we were over the three-quarter bushel mark and lauding each other for our skill and luck. Of course at that same point the tidal current died, as did the crab movement. It took more than two hours to finish, but we were back at the ramp by noon with a bulging bushel of the blue beauties.

There is something special about the Chesapeake Bay blue crab. And there is definitely something special about catching them and cooking them up yourself. For our family and friends, everything else is a distant second, and I couldn't think of a better way to celebrate my birthday.

TRY IT YOURSELF

Recreational crabbing on the Chesapeake is an especially egalitarian affair. Anyone and everyone can do it with little specialized equipment or preparation. You don't even have to have a license if you keep to a two-dozen-per-person possession limit.

While I generally work a trotline measuring about 900 feet, I will often go the ball-of-twine approach for its simplicity and casual nature. A ball of cotton twine for hand lines, a few chicken necks, a long-handled crab net and an airy basket to keep them in is all you need.

A local pier or bulkhead will generally provide access to crabbing waters. A flood tide, early morning arrival and multiple lines increase your chances of success. Crabs drift and swim with that current in their constant search for food. The better the water movement is over and around your baits, the more the chances for good numbers of crabs.

Tie a neck on each line. When a hungry crab—and crabs are always hungry—finds the tasty morsel, it will try to swim off with it. This straightens out the length of twine, alerting the waiting crabber. Grasp the line delicately, and gently retrieve until the crab is visible. Then ease into position. Start with the net below the crab, for it will flee downward, and make a quick scoop. A blue crab is lightning fast in the water.

Crab traps are also efficient devices. Baited with chicken necks or pieces of fish, they are lowered to the bottom on a cord. When they are pulled up, the devices close, trapping crabs inside. Traps have the benefit of working in deeper water and off higher piers and bulkheads. They also don't require quite the luck and net skill as simpler crab lines.

Assuming the crabber is fortunate and the prize meets the minimum size of five inches point to point (5.25 after July 14), your dinner is on its way to your table.

Store your catch in a split wood bushel basket or ventilated plastic basket. Good air circulation is essential. Buckets and coolers doom a crab to an early demise, rendering it ineligible for dinner. Dead crabs must never be cooked. Kept cool in the shade or in an air-conditioned room, blue crabs will live for 24 hours or more.

CATCH 'EM, COOK 'EM, EAT 'EM

Back at the house, Vince and I accepted our spouses' surprised congratulations, settled our gear and cleaned up. I took a birthday nap, leaving the interim preparations in the hands of my sainted wife, Deb, and Tarin Fuller, the other half of the couple from New Jersey. By six that evening, the dining room table had been cleared and protected with multiple layers of newspaper. The mallets and knives, rolls of paper towels and dishes of spices were ready to go. It was time for cooking.

I immerse crabs in heavily iced water prior to cooking. It will wash off sand, and after about five minutes in this frigid bath, even the hardiest crab will become dormant. Chilled crabs can be easily handled and stacked compact into a steamer. The crabs will not regain consciousness during cooking, hence will not throw their claws or legs.

My youngest son, Robert, had taken on the task of assembling the propane tank and gas burner, tongs, cardboard platters and adding in just the right mixture of equal parts beer and water with a pour of vinegar. Outside in the yard, my old crab cooker, fashioned from a stainless steel beer keg, was spurting steam and the unmistakable aroma of Maryland bliss: hot crabs.

Twenty minutes of steam time is enough to complete the job; more than 30 minutes risks making the crab meat mushy.

They should be bright red; crabs of a darker color indicate more cooking time is needed.

Just as the feast was almost ready, our middle boy, Harrison, arrived from Baltimore, having finally extricated himself from the weekend traffic.

The pile of hot, fat crabs, heavily dosed with that familiar, steaming spice mixture, was soon heaped on the newspaper-covered dining room table, a sight as beautiful and fragrant as anything ever beheld.

Somehow we all got seated, a platter of steamed corn and salad miraculously appeared, cold beverages were distributed, a bottle of birthday champagne popped and the meal commenced.

As I looked around the room at what had transpired in my home, I wished that living on the Chesapeake Bay would forever be just like this for all my family and friends. I silently thanked the heavens for this unique and delicious bounty.

Eliyahu Yosef Parypa/Shutterstock

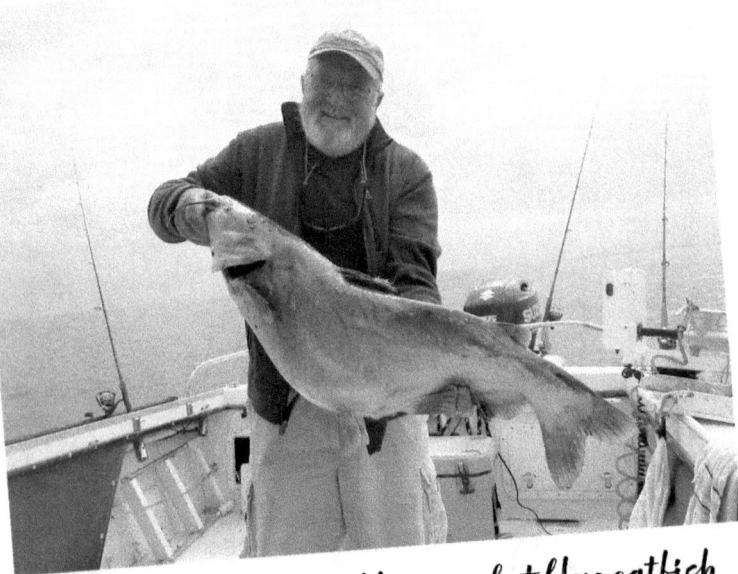

Frank Tuma shows off a very fat blue catfish.

Catch What's Biting

SNAKEHEADS AND CATFISH ARE PLENTIFUL

Over Memorial Day weekend, I overheard a new, amusing joke.

Question: Why are snakeheads and catfish the most numerous fish we're catching?

Answer: Because they're the only two species Maryland Department of Natural Resources hasn't tried to help.

That might unfairly criticize the efforts of our Natural Resources Department on other species. But there's truth in it, and that's that neither species needs a fishery management plan to prosper. Both are invasive species and in recent years have become abundant and, on the plus side, they're good eating.

Snakeheads originated in Asia and were introduced to the Bay as released aquarium fish. Blue catfish are native to the Mississippi and were introduced to the James River by the state of Virginia as a sport species. Their ability to migrate to the Chesapeake came as a surprise.

Angling for both species is fairly straightforward, and neither is hook-shy or difficult to catch once located.

SNAKEHEAD STRATEGIES

Snakeheads have spread to the fresher areas of just about all the tributaries. They have a profound fondness for frogs. If you can locate waters with a healthy sprinkling of lily pads, try twitching a Zoom Horny Toad or similar soft-plastic subsurface frog bait along any channel you find in the pads. Pause your retrieve often.

If the vegetation is too thick to swim a bait under the surface, throw a floating weedless frog on top and move it slowly in jerks with long pauses. With either surface or subsurface baits, wait until you feel the pull of the fish on your line before you strike. Explosions of water in the pads or milfoil won't produce a hookup on their own, and your reaction to the disturbance will pull the lure away from the fish and alert it to your intentions.

Swimming a bull minnow or any small fish under a bobber near the same vegetation or around any type of structure can also produce. Crank-and-jerk baits resembling silverside minnows, peanut bunker or any small fish will also draw attacks. Snakeheads are ambush predators. Their mouthful of pointed teeth is intended for grasping and usually will not sever a mono leader of 10 pounds or more.

When you are fishing near heavy vegetation of this type, using a 30-pound test or over-braid like Power Pro for your main line is a good idea. The snakeheads can often grow above 15 pounds. When hooked, these powerful fish immediately bore into the densest cover available. You'll need braid's narrow diameter, vegetation-severing power and high breaking strength to muscle them out.

CATFISHING

Baitfishing for blue cats is simple. If you're throwing spinner baits for perch or casting small soft plastic jerk-baits for shallow-water rockfish, catfish may bite as well. You can also chum for them just as you would for rockfish. Or you can bottom fish with menhaden, cut perch, cut spot, crab, night-crawlers, bloodworms, clams or live minnows. Catfish are not picky and will even ingest chicken livers, chicken pieces, cut eel, doughballs and most any commercial catfish bait.

Keep a net handy, for both these species are extra slippery. Snakeheads are armed with sharp teeth and can swim backwards as well as forwards. Remember that fact when you try to lead them into your net. The catfish have sharp dorsal, pectoral and anal fins that hold some painful toxins, so be careful getting them out of the net.

Both species will need to be skinned before cleaning. After that has been accomplished, it's a simple job to cut out the fillets as they have few bones.

My favorite recipe for both is to cut the meat into bite-sized pieces, dip them in a sticky mixture of flour and beer, roll them in Panko (Japanese bread crumbs) and fry them in a heavy skillet with about a half-inch of hot, almost smoking, peanut oil.

Beer is an excellent adult beverage for this fry up. I particularly enjoy a craft-brewed ale such as Fordham's Copperhead or Devil's Backbone Striped Bass, though in this case the latter has just the slightest aftertaste of irony.

Harrison Doyle caught this 25 - inch rockfish live-lining.

The Key to Catching Fish

FISHING IS UNPREDICTABLE,
SO YOU NEED TO BE ABLE TO ADAPT

We were drifting inside of the green channel marker off Podickery Point when my son got a quizzical look on his face. Staring at the rapidly turning spool of his reel, Harrison said, "I think I'm hung up."

"No, I don't think so," I replied. "Give it a minute." The spool stopped for a beat, then started up again even faster.

IF AT FIRST

I had promised my middle son success on some nice rockfish, forgetting that if you wish to amuse the fish gods, simply announce your plans. We intended to drift soft crab, based on a hot tip from a charter boat skipper who had scored exceedingly well the day before.

Perfect, I thought, on waking. I knew just where the fish would likely be that morning and just what bait to use. But when I began my early-hour quest for crab, source after source said, sorry, sold out. I feared that if the rockfish were keying on soft crab, anything else would be a very distant second choice.

At 10 a.m., armed only with a bag of scraggly bloodworms purchased in desperation, we finally motored out to try something else.

It took a half-hour to find some likely marks off the edge of a nearby river channel before we could drop down pieces of worm on our No. 6 hooks. Feeling the tic-tic-tic of our rigs' sinkers bouncing over shell bottom was reassuring, and soon we were swinging a couple of 4-to-5-inch perch on board. They would make fine live-lining baits in these early weeks of the season before the Norfolk spot showed up and took over as the rockfish's favorite meal.

I filled our live well, hooked up the aerator and deposited the small baitfish with a sense of relief. Perhaps we could tempt some rockfish to eat after all.

Once we had a dozen small perch in our well, we headed for the Bay Bridge. It was almost noon, and the sun was bright and high. Not the best of conditions, but it would have to do.

About half way to our destination, we approached a cluster of boats sitting on chum slicks. Their anchor lines looked slack, and the postures of the anglers slumped in their craft suggested things had not been going well.

As we skirted the fleet, I happened to glance down at my finder screen where some good marks strongly suggested rockfish. They were suspended from 10 to 15 feet over a 30-foot bottom. Our frisky perch just might prove tempting to them.

We had our live-lining outfits rigged and ready to go, so in no time, two lively baitfish were swimming down. Periodically boosting the perch into the rockfish danger zone, we slowly drifted along while staying clear of the anchored boats and pushed by a mild breeze.

Within just a few minutes, Harrison had his first run. When he slowly tightened the line, remembering we were using circle hooks, he came tight to the fish as the hook found purchase in the corner of its mouth. The rod bent to the corks and the drag began to hiss as the mono poured out. It was a good fish and a solid hookup. After several minutes of a lively battle, we had a 29-inch striper in the net, then buried in ice.

Shortly after, I had a fat and healthy 25-incher join the bigger fish in the same box.

Those two fish, as it turned out, were indeed blessings as our finder screen then went empty. The school had fled for parts unknown.

We cruised likely looking areas for another hour or more with no results and finally decided to declare victory and head back to the ramp to enjoy a late lunch. We had tempted the fish gods enough for one day.

Christian St. Holmes stands to cast as dusk settles in.

The Storm vs the Rockfish

WHICH COMES FIRST IS THE QUESTION
OF MANY A SUMMER NIGHT

The light wind brought a welcome coolness to my cheeks as I drifted ever closer to the ripline at the mouth of the river. I lifted from the live well a struggling spot already pinned just in front of the dorsal with a light-wire 6/0 circle hook. It was full dark on a very quiet evening, and I was by myself.

One of the better times to fish in summer's heat is after dark. You will have scant company. And on the right night with the right tide there can be some incredible action.

The silence can be a little spooky.

There is another source of tension. Scanning the darkness, I strained my eyes for lightning. A summertime squall on the Bay is not to be trifled with.

Reviewing weather radar earlier, I had decided this would be a good fishing night as the screen scan was free of storm activity. Still, an intense burst of nasty weather could move in quickly. It's impossible to judge a squall's direction in the dark. So any sign would send me scurrying home. Tonight it was so far, so good.

Lowering the spot into the water, I let the small fish have its head. As I drifted at the mouth of my favorite tributary, I kept one eye glued to my fish-finder's screen, dimmed so it didn't cancel out my night vision or light up the skiff. The tidal current and light breeze were coordinated tonight; both were complementing rather than complicating my fishing,

As high flood approached, I hoped that a school of rockfish would venture in for the small spot and perch that teemed the bottom here the last few days. From the look of my screen, my hope seemed to be coming true.

Soon, things were percolating. The first indication was frantic rushes by my small baitfish. I had set my reel's casting tension extra-light, offering little impediment to the spot's effort to evade any predator.

Rockfish are excellent night hunters. I wouldn't be surprised that they find the majority of their summer sustenance in the dark. Now they were out hunting. My line soon pulsed with a strong relentless power. I put my reel in gear and let the line come tight. Curbing the urge to set the hook, I let the fish exert its force against my rod until it bent over hard and I was sure the circle hook had found its mark.

Rewarded by the hissing sound of a lot of line being pulled off into the dark against my drag, I patiently let the fish tire itself out. Then off in the distance, a brief, flickering glimmer alarmed me. A rumble followed. I quickly led the fish into my net.

Icing it down and setting my rod back in the rack, I fired up the Yamaha and set course for the ramp. Within a half an hour, I was enjoying a cold adult tinned beverage while listening to the thunder boom and rain pour down my home's eaves.

A cooling summer storm is better enjoyed from the comforts of home than from the cockpit of a rain-drenched and storm-tossed skiff.

JENG BO YUAN/Shutterstock.

What's at the End of the Line?

A BIG, POWERFUL SURPRISE

The rod tip dipped, then dipped again. Reaching out, my longtime friend Sandy Sempliner eased the rod from its holder. His reel spool then began to turn slowly. Thumbing it lightly, he tried to determine if extra tidal current was providing the force or if a crafty fish down below was making off with his bait. The pull on the line increased, and the spool blurred.

Sandy was sure now that something big had his hunk of menhaden. Giving it half dozen or so additional seconds, he finally threw the reel into gear. Pointing the rod directly at the fish, he cranked until the line came tight, then slammed the rod back hard, hammering home the hook. The heavy-action rod bent down into the corks. The fight was on.

The adrenaline that a big fish starts up in your body can be exhilarating. Sandy's grin was as wide as his face, his eyes bright with excitement. The reel's drag was ripping now and his rod, bending hard over, was making that creaking sound that sometimes comes just before the graphite shaft blows into a thousand shards. He eased up and let the fish run.

The big fish cut across far behind the stern of our skiff as I rushed to get other trailing lines out of the way. Then the fish came toward the surface. We looked aft, expecting to see the explosion of a silvery striped flank, but in the distance there only appeared broad brown wing tip cutting through the surface with a long whip-like tail trailing behind. It was a cownose ray.

It wasn't the trophy we thought. However, having already spent almost three hours fishing without a nibble, we welcomed the hook-up as a break from the morning's monotony.

Over long and laborious minutes, my friend finally worked the brute close enough to the boat to release it. I had intended to remove the hook. But our quarry had other ideas, and I certainly wanted no part of the serrated, toxin-laden spike poised at the base of its thrashing tail.

I cut the leader as close to the winged monster as I could and watched as it slowly made its way back into the depths from which we had disturbed it. Sandy had never caught a ray before and was impressed with its power. I had to agree it was a graceful and handsome creature.

THE BAY'S RAYS

European explorers first encountered cownose rays in 1608. Near the mouth of the Chesapeake, Captain John Smith attempted to spear the specimen with his sword. In the struggle, he was hit in the shoulder by the ray's stinger.

Some current piscatorial literature describes the toxin as "a weak venom that causes symptoms similar to that of a bee sting." Smith's crew, observing the captain's long and extreme agony, were so sure he was going to die that they dug his grave.

Captain Smith survived the ordeal and ate the ray. The place it all happened is still called Stingray Point, named for that morning.

Schools of cownose rays, sometimes numbering in the thousands, travel down the Atlantic Coast to visit the Chesapeake every summer, coming all the way up past the

Patapsco River. They dine on young oysters, clams and mussels, while tormenting anglers by eating baits meant for other species.

The rays feed and mate in the shallows during these warmer months and also give live birth to baby rays conceived the previous year. The pups have a wingspread of about 12 inches.

This was not quite the experience we were looking for, but it did have its moments. The brute power of the rays tested our tackle and our knot-tying before finally sending us packing.

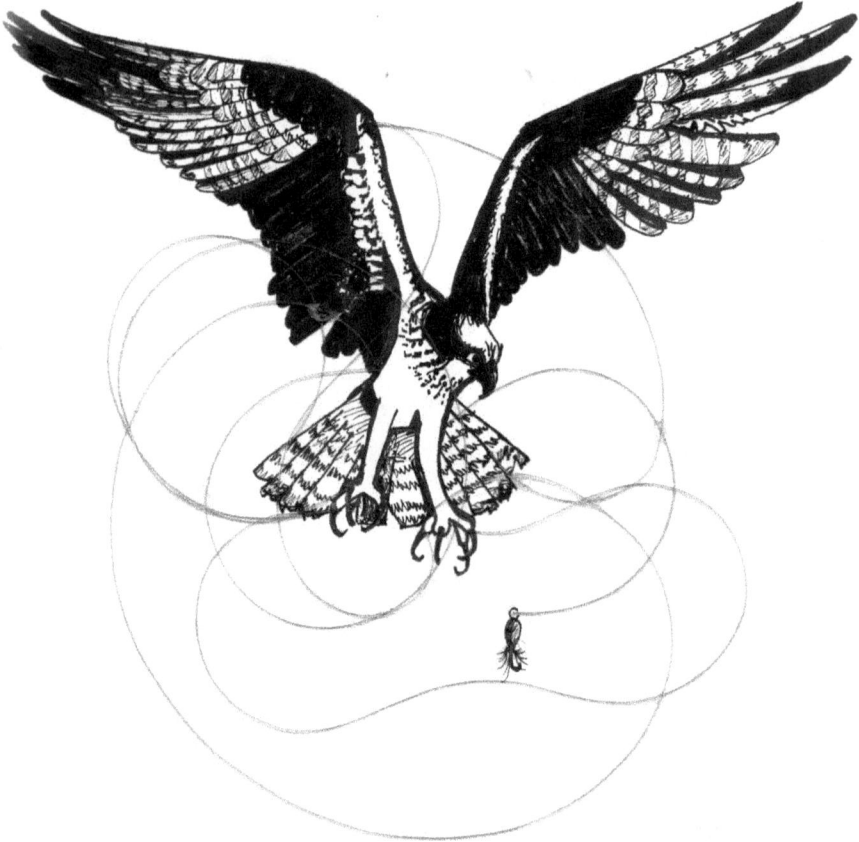

Osprey Unbound

Taking a stroll after an early dinner, Judy Barrett and her husband Dick saw the makings of a fable for our times.

An osprey was struggling in the channel, entangled in monofilament line trailing from a fish it had caught. The bird could not get airborne. After straining on the water for some time, it managed to make its way to the service dock where Judy and Dick stood watching.

Observing the osprey's plight, an attendant ran for a landing net while the bird huddled patiently below. He scooped up the bird and deposited it on the dock.

The big fish hawk then sat quietly while the courageous, and somewhat amazed, attendant untangled the monofilament from its wings and talons. At no time did the bird protest or resist the efforts of the young man helping it.

Finally clear of the line, the bird stood up, calmly shook itself, looked around and took back to the air.

It was an amazing exercise of trust by both parties. Perhaps we can all get along after all.

July

Proof of the pudding:
Doyle caught this rockfish at night, on his fly rod.

Night on the Chesapeake

WITHOUT CROWDS OR VISION, YOU FISH BY FEEL

The word has been out for some time now. This rocky point and its shoal waters where good stripers have been visiting in the late afternoon are not a secret any more. An hour or before dusk, the skiffs begin to motor in and anchor up.

The clank of the Danforth anchors as they are dropped, sometimes hurled, into the water, echoes noisily. Apparently there's an actual party on board a nearby boat; at least two other conversations carry across the water.

In spite of the racket, a pod of fish shows. Anxious anglers cast baits and lures. Some are rewarded. Shouts of excitement ring out, nets are wildly displayed and the occasional splashes of conquered rockfish can be heard within this scattered, impromptu fleet.

I make some casts with my fly rod, but my heart isn't in it. My popper gets no attention anyway. The action becomes sporadic for another half-hour. As daylight dies, the navigation lights begin to blink on, and one by one the other boats fire up and head for home. It gets darker. Finally I am alone.

Nothing happens immediately, but then it usually doesn't. Change is going on. The water gets quieter and blacker. The sounds soften and expand. You begin to hear things that weren't there a while ago: small pops; a quiet splash; waves suddenly audible against the distant rocks.

With a sliver of the moon now showing, a few baitfish frolic, jumping over drifting twigs and debris just for the joy of it. The tidal current hissing against the hull becomes mesmerizing.

This is an older Chesapeake that is descending, a wild, big water with real adventure waiting just beneath its dark surface.

Fly fishing at night always tests my patience and control. Removing my sandals, I step up on the casting deck. Checking my line to be sure it's still stretched out and free of kinks and coils, I strip it onto the deck. I can feel it immediately trying to sneak under my feet; I do my best to keep it clear.

I'm using a heavily dressed black-streamer fly now. It's weighted and tied so the hook point rides up and won't foul on the submerged rocks. How a striper can so easily find a three-inch black fly against a murky bottom in the dark of the night is beyond my reasoning. But night fishing, this kind anyway, has little to do with logic or reason.

It's hard to throw a fly now because you can't see your loop form as you cast. You've got to relax and feel the rod flex as the line moves through the air. Maintaining timing and getting your cast out becomes a serious challenge. Forcing things doesn't help. So you get relaxed. You have to.

I work my line into the dark and make my throw. The line shoots out; then I feel the tide pulling it across its flow and down into the depths. My long, slender rod dips and undulates with the moving water, and I can imagine the fly sliding and curling along the rocky bottom.

A peacefulness that had eluded me all week finally slips into place. A deep breath helps my focus, and, as the line straightens out in the distant blackness, I hold it in the current for a moment and let the fly swim.

When the hit comes, I'm surprised, as if a fish were the farthest thing from my mind. I strike back hard, pulling my rod into my hip with the line clenched against the cork grip.

It's a good striper, heavy. I hear it crash up through the surface of the night water as it bolts. The coils of loose fly line leap off the deck and hiss through the guides. I try desperately to maintain line tension, and I'm terrified something will knot up or go wrong. Then, finally, the fish is on the reel.

It's a weathered Billy Pate salmon model that's probably caught a couple of hundred fish before it came to me. The reel's drag is making a sweet, soft hum, and the sound reassures me as the bass continues to run off in the dark. Forcing my deeply bent rod high and off to the side, I carefully add finger pressure to the rim of the whirling spool. It's old and smooth and warms at my touch.

I hear the fish broach again somewhere off in the blackness. The stars, high over the water, appear suddenly brighter. I want this moment to go on forever.

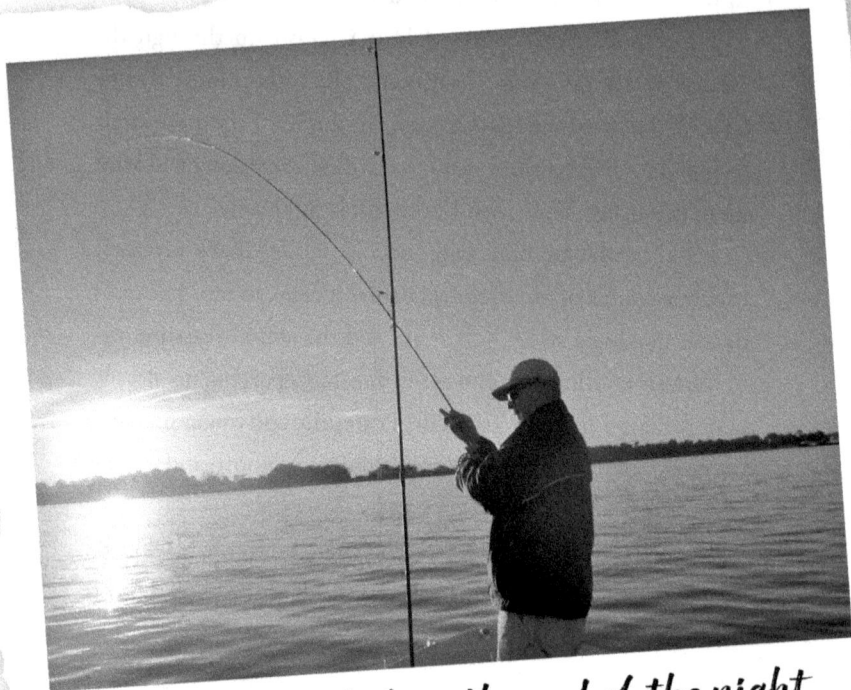

Settling in to fish in the cool of the night.

Hot Times on the Bay

TAKE CARE OF YOURSELF AND THE FISH

Temperatures flirting with triple digits can mean difficult times on the Chesapeake, not only for anglers but also for the fish.

The young and old are the most susceptible to heatstroke. But everyone needs to be aware of the danger, as it can be fatal.

Heatstroke often gives no warning, quickly rendering you unconscious. So take special precautions if fishing or paddling solo. Staying hydrated—continually drinking water—is a must when the temperatures go above the 80s. It would be particularly foolish for the solo adventurer to fail to don a life jacket.

Should you experience confusion, dizziness or unusual weakness during these hot days, immediately seek cooler conditions and slowly ingest cold drinks to lower your core body temperature. If the symptoms or the sufferer begins to lose consciousness, seek emergency medical care promptly. And always keep foremost in mind the most common symptom of heat exhaustion: confused decision making.

Fish also are at risk during high temperatures. Catch-and-release fishing should be avoided once the temperature reaches the 80-degree mark. Mortality skyrockets for rockfish (particularly for those 24-inches and longer) hooked during these hot-weather days, often despite best efforts to quickly release them.

A number of strategics will minimize exposure to the sun's effects for both the fish and you. First, target the wee hours from first light until 10 a.m. and from 6 p.m. until last light. Those hours are also prime times for the best bite.

Nighttime fishing is also an option for the more adventurous —as long as you are completely familiar with areas to be fished and prepared with good communications, extra flashlights, batteries, cold refreshments, a GPS and a fishing plan with specific locations in the hands of someone on shore. Put on your life jacket when you're out on the water at night.

Rockfish are particularly active after dark and will often haunt shallower water in search of prey. I can attest that a striped bass will locate and inhale even a black fly or lure fished on a moonless night with no trouble. Your best strategy is to exercise extreme care and silence in your approach.

However it is illegal to be in possession of rockfish while angling after 12 midnight and before 5 a.m. The rule applies to shore as well as on-water anglers.

Croaker and sea trout are also very active after dark, often more so than any time during the day, and will move into shallower water and feed very aggressively. Use crab, bloodworms or shrimp as bait. Sea trout are suckers for Assassin-type soft jigs fished slowly near the bottom.

White perch in the larger sizes will likewise remain active in the darker hours. Searching with noise-producing lures, including one-eighth and one-quarter ounce Rat-L-Traps, is particularly productive and can often attract marauding rockfish, a definite challenge if you're using ultra-light tackle.

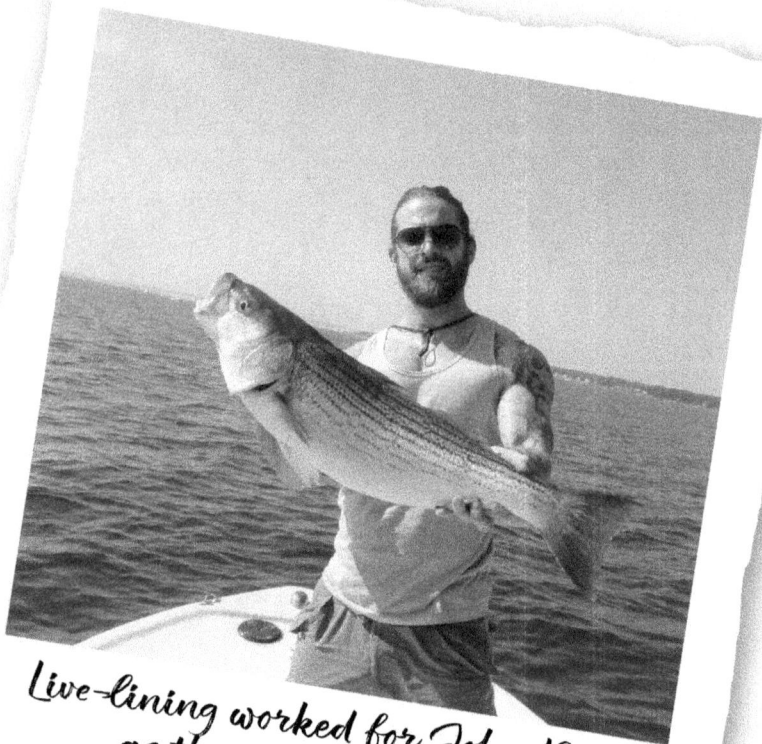

Live-lining worked for John Doyle, as this rockfish shows.

There's More Than One Way to Catch a Rockfish

LIVE-LINING CAN BEAT CHUMMING—WITHOUT THE STINK

As I flipped my live perch over the side, my son did the same. Hoping that we would not have to wait too long for action, I let the small baitfish swim down and away from the boat. The lines streamed aft and out to port as a light wind pushed our skiff slowly over the calm water.

Within a few seconds, my line was feeding out unusually fast. I glanced around for orientation to gauge just how fast the tide was moving. My son John called, "Dad, your line is crossing over mine," but when I tried to check its flow, I discovered it wasn't the current that was pulling out my baitfish. It was something far stronger.

"I'm getting a run already. Something took my bait," I said. "You'll have to bring your line in."

"I can't. I have a fish on," John answered. His rod was bent to the corks, and line was pouring off his spool.

Throwing my reel in gear, I came tight to my fish to the same effect: My rod bent down and a strong rockfish headed out and away. I did my best to keep my line from crossing my son's. For long moments it was a delightfully difficult situation.

Laughing and dodging around each other as we finally got separation, I had to warn John to push his rod tip deep underwater to keep his line clear of our motor's lower unit. His fish had turned and managed to angle his line under the hull.

I thought about raising the motor in assistance, then decided my hands were full. It was every man for himself.

The response had turned us optimistic. When we arrived, I had been alarmed to see more than 50 fishing craft clustered in the area. Fortunately, most of the others were trolling or anchored and fishing bait. Neither would interfere with our live-lining tactics, and we would have both of our limits in less than half an hour.

LESSONS IN TACKLE, BAIT AND READING THE WATER

Live-lining is an exciting and less odorous enterprise than chumming. It is also, under the proper circumstances, more productive.

I call my switch from chumming accidental—or fortuitous. Here's how it happened. A week or so into the summer season as the trophy season ended, I had reconnoitered a substantial school of 5-inch and under white perch. While the best baitfish are Norfolk spot 4 to 6 inches long, until they appear, small white perch will also do the trick. I took their appearance as an omen that it might be time to start live-lining.

So I got out my portable live well and made sure it was operating. Boat live wells are designed for just this sort of thing, but aerated buckets can work as well. The aerator must be heavy duty (12 volt) to manage more than a half dozen baitfish for long periods. Many baitfish species have a poor tolerance for low oxygen and become exhausted or expire if the levels in your container become too low.

Bait-casting outfits are designed specifically for this technique. Spin outfits, particularly the bait-runner models, do the job just as effectively. I use the same tackle I employ for chumming but with different terminal setups. For live-lining, I prefer to use lighter leaders, no more than 20-pound-test fluorocarbon, connected to the main line with a black-finished stainless-steel ball-bearing swivel. Around bridge supports, piers or lighthouses I move up to 30-pound fluoro leaders because of the added hazards of barnacles on the man-made structure.

My favorite main line is standard high-quality monofilament. Hook preferences run from size 7/0 and larger non-offset circle hooks.

Change baits often. A tired perch or spot does not usually draw a predator's interest. They want the lively ones.

Thus equipped, you're ready to read the water.

As I prefer to live-line without weight, letting the bait fish swim down on its own and hold there, I've found the most productive tidal phases to be the slower portions of the tidal flows. The first hour and a half of moving current or the last hour and a half allow my baitfish to get deep to attract our quarry.

When tidal current is low, live-lining can be very effective for drifting around bridge supports or specific bottom structure such as rock piles, pipelines or cable crossings, even likely marks suspended in more open water.

When the currents or the wind pick up, a different approach becomes advantageous.

It is difficult to drift-fish structure or open water with stiff winds or hard-running tidal currents. You cannot stay in productive areas, the boat is hard to control and your baits are too quickly carried away from the sweet spot. In these conditions, the best strategy is to anchor up so that the boat trails near the location you wish to fish. Anchoring is also a good idea if you've got a school in a static location or if you intend to chum the fish to your boat.

You may also need to add some weight to your line, using a live-lining rig with a sliding sinker to get the fish at the proper depth. The baitfish should be hooked through the nose or both lips for a more natural presentation down in the water column. Hooked in this way, it doesn't have to struggle to keep oriented to the current and will stay frisky much longer.

In all cases, when you feel a rockfish take hold of your live baitfish you must let it run unimpeded. If the striper feels any resistance, particularly a larger, smarter rockfish, it will spit the bait. Waiting a long eight or nine count while the striper swims off will allow the fish to move the bait into the back of its mouth and give you the best chance of a good hook set.

Do not attempt to horse a fish in the last few feet or snub a last-minute dash for the bottom. Be patient, set your drag on the light side, let them run and you'll land 'em all—as we did that day.

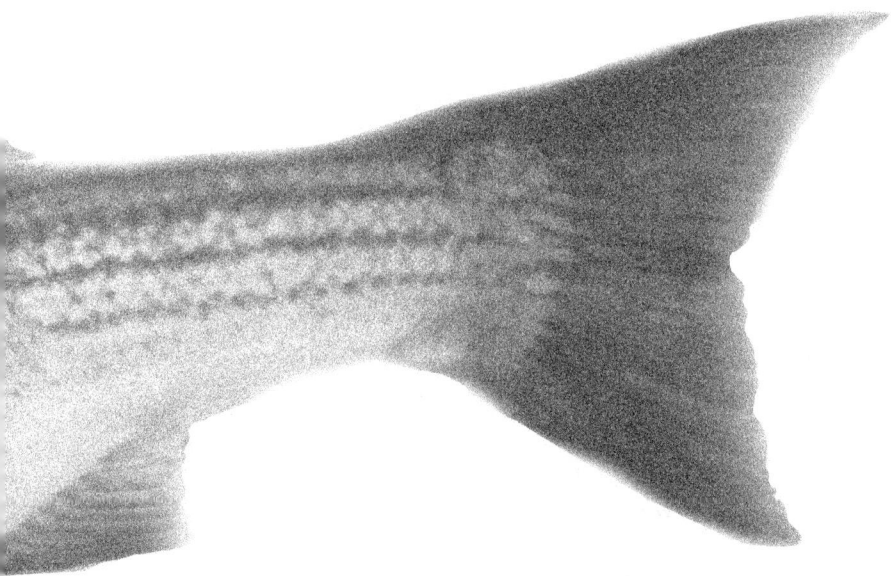

Robert Doyle lured from teenage pursuits by a 23 - inch rockfish.

Fishing for Teenagers—

YOU'LL BE FIGHTING THE LURE OF VIDEO GAMES, SKATEBOARDING AND NEWFOUND FRIENDS

The reel spool started to turn quickly. In the twilight it took a second or two for me to note the movement. It slowed for just a beat, then the drag hissed as line accelerated through the guides. My alert level moved into the red zone.

I spoke quietly to my young teenage son, who had been concentrating on getting the last trail mix bar out of its wrapper.

"Hey, Robert, fish on. Do you want it?"

"Yes," he replied, not nearly so quietly, and reached up to take the rod out of the holder. I cautioned him to let the fish have the bait. But shortly he could stand it no longer, threw the reel into gear and poised the rod. I crossed my fingers.

We had been live-lining small perch for only about 20 minutes just inside the river mouth. But evening had already fallen. It had taken us longer than anticipated to catch a sufficient supply of small perch from nearby jetties, and now we were trying to concentrate on the good stuff: getting a striped bass to eat one of our perch. Apparently that was now happening.

At first, the line just came taut. For a second, I feared the fish had dropped the bait. Then the rod tip jerked down, and Rob hauled back. The battle was on.

"It's not going to spit the perch out, is it?" he asked after the first strong run, as the fish started a big half circle.

"Naw, he's got it good," I said. But more than a few had given me the slip by doing just that. I said a small prayer.

Long minutes later, Robert had worked it nearer and we could see by the heavy surges of water when it surfaced that it was a good fish. The fight went on. Twice, then three times, Robert got it almost close enough for my net. But each time it moved off against the drag. This was getting a little too tense.

At last Robert got its head up as it neared the boat, and I got the net just right. He was ours. It was a nice fish, about 22 or 23 inches, its brightly striped body glistening in the anchor light that now softly illuminated our boat.

It had been a while since Robert and I had been on a fishing trip together. I had been trying to get him out. But the lure of video games, skateboarding and newfound friendship occupied his time much of the summer. Then he decided he needed to go fishing. I hastened to accommodate him.

NOT THIS FISH BUT THE NEXT ONE

We both admired the fish as I removed it from the folds of the net. But something wasn't right. Just above the anal fin was a large and unmistakable crimson stain reaching almost to its tail. It had a bacterial infection. Not good. Not good at all.

"Robert, this fish had got to go back. It's got a skin infection," I told him.

He wanted to keep it anyway. But when I asked if he thought he would eat it, he relented.

"There's a good chance that when the colder weather comes, the sores will heal and the fish will become healthy again," I explained.

"Yeah, he'll be even bigger next year," my son replied.

I got one quick picture before Rob eased the fish over the side and sent it on its way. Then we both rinsed our hands.

We swam a few more perch as our fish finder purred with telltale marks. But the fish had stopped biting.

Then the wind picked up, and the tide started to slack. We pulled up a short while later. On the cruise back to the docks, my son recounted his exploits in picking up our perch supply as well as catching the only eligible keeper. He had landed two or three fish to each of mine, and he clearly enjoyed recounting the superior skill involved. I agreed wholeheartedly.

The next evening, Robert cajoled my wife into accompanying him in our double kayak to a nearby creek. He was intent on laying in a supply of nice-sized live perch so that we would not have to waste so much time when we went out for another try at a rockfish. He was suddenly possessed with getting a big one that he can keep. I plan to be there.

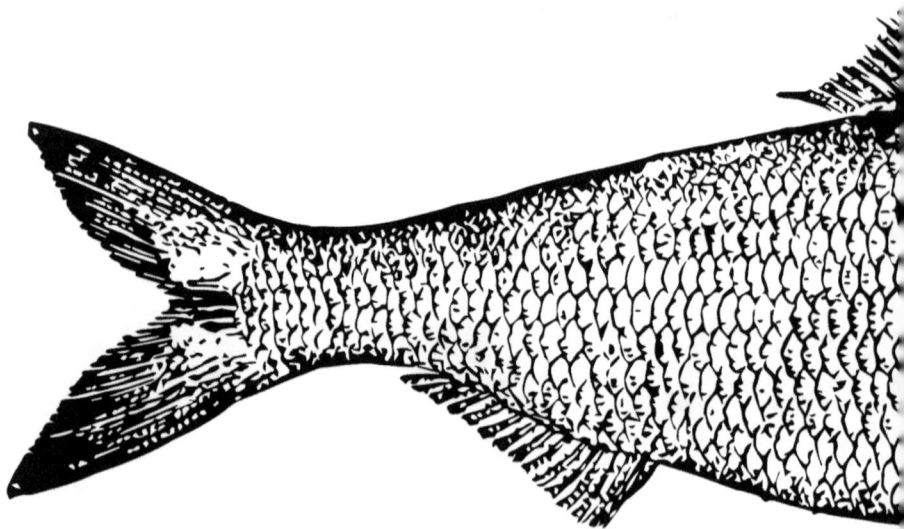

August

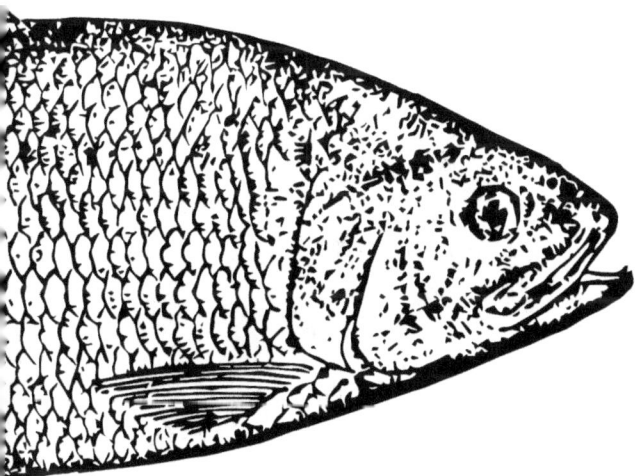

Mike Fiore celebrates his citation black perch.

Ever Caught a Black Perch?

THIS HARD FIGHTER IS INCOMPARABLE ON THE TABLE

My memory of black perch begins quite a few years ago on the Eastern Shore. I was fishing out of Crisfield in the early 1970s with the first and only fly-fishing guide on the Chesapeake, Doug Carson. I had searched out Doug with some difficulty by calling everyone in the Eastern Shore phonebook with the last name of Carson. Doug had been taught fly rod techniques personally by Lefty Kreh, eventually the most famous fly rod man in America, and Lefty had named Doug in an early article or two.

I had looped out a long cast with a small, white marabou streamer to a sunken rock jetty off Janes Island and had come tight with what I assumed was another rowdy schoolie rock.

As I fought the fish near the boat, Doug reached over, grabbed my leader and flipped the chunky devil into the skiff remarking, "Nice black perch. Didn't want you to lose that one."

Looking at the dark, black-backed fish flopping all over the deck I said, "Isn't that a white perch?"

"Yeah, but around here we call the big ones black perch. The little ones are whites," Doug replied.

That still makes a lot of sense to me.

Just last week, searching for Norfolk spot for live-lining to striped bass, I had stumbled on a gathering of those big black-backed perch. They were incredibly thick-bodied, and the few that I had caught measured around 11 inches. Then I had abandoned them to continue my search for bait-sized spot (4- to 6-inch), a search that proved ultimately unsuccessful.

The memory of those big perch haunted me for days. Now I was back for a rematch with the black-backed devils and armed to the teeth for what I, and many other fervent anglers, consider one of the best-tasting and hardest-fighting treasures of the Chesapeake.

DRESSING FOR SUCCESS

On the deck of my 15-foot skiff were arranged three light spin rods, much more efficient than fly rods for catching white perch in numbers. My goal this time was a family perch fry, and the hefty fish I was seeking would undoubtedly prove almost as sporting on light spin tackle as they would have on a fly rod.

My long, 6-foot 9-inch rod had 6-pound ultra-thin mono spooled on its reel and sported a one-sixth-ounce Super Rooster Tail lure in the Clown Coach Dog pattern. That singular bait has become, over the last half-dozen years, the pre-eminent Bay lure for coaxing white perch out of the shore-bound structure they sometimes prefer this time of season.

With that rod's length and that lure, I had the perfect long-range searching tool. Working from a distance and drifting the areas around those where I had originally encountered the big guys, I hoped to encounter them again. Once I had, I would quietly move up, anchor and work them over.

The two shorter rods, 5½-footers, were fixed with 8-pound-test line for better dealing with the abrasion of the heavy, rock-strewn structure. They had different lures tied on. White perch won't hesitate to hammer the Rooster Tail, but after it's been presented to a particular area a number of times, interest in it will decrease—though numerous fish may still be present.

Switching to another pattern or type of lure will often regain their interest and in some cases result in triggering strikes from even bigger fish. I have found, particularly, that even after rejecting other artificials, often a jumbo perch can't resist a small, noisy crank bait.

So while one of the other rods was simply adorned with another pattern of spinner bait, I had the second rigged with a blue-backed, chrome-sided Rat-L-Trap in one-eighth-ounce. That tiny plug had enticed vicious strikes from some jumbo perch in the past. I hoped it would again today.

I also carried a small, long-handled crab net for scooping the delicate-mouthed, hard-fighting devils as they neared the boat. Although Doug Carson didn't hesitate to line-flip that big black into his boat 30-some years ago, a 12-inch perch back in those days and in that neck of the woods was no big thing. Today in the mid-Bay, if I lost one that size at skiff-side, it would be cause for tears.

Just once in a great while a plan works out perfectly. This one did it in spades, or more accurately, in an ice chest of fine black perch. Finding the jumbos still close to where I first encountered them a week ago, over the course of two hours I tangled with countless numbers of tough-fighting fish—to the point of a sore wrist and an aching arm.

One was a particularly formidable adversary. Boring for deep water in an extended, measured run, the perch then paused and just plain refused to budge. I lifted my rod and tried to pull him toward the surface but found it almost impossible to gain line.

Having lost a number of big perch trying to out-muscle them, I patiently kept a deep bend in my stick. Eventually the fish began to move, steadily and away. Early in the battle I was suspicious that the rascal was a rockfish in disguise, but its steady, determined runs and thumping head shakes convinced me that it was an old, thick-shouldered black back.

Netting the beast as it finally emerged from the depths, I was still astonished by its size. Measured from the fork in its tail to the tip of the nose, it registered a solid 13¾ inches, my personal best in 35 years of fishing the Chesapeake.

As contrast, it would take a rockfish of more than 36 inches on light tackle to equal the thrill of landing this outsized perch, indeed a trophy.

A dozen and a half of the nicer ones, all weighing about a pound each and measuring up to 12 inches, plus this lunker, I put on ice. It proved a memorable day and an even more memorable dinner. Though it wasn't done on a fly rod, I think Doug would still have been proud of me.

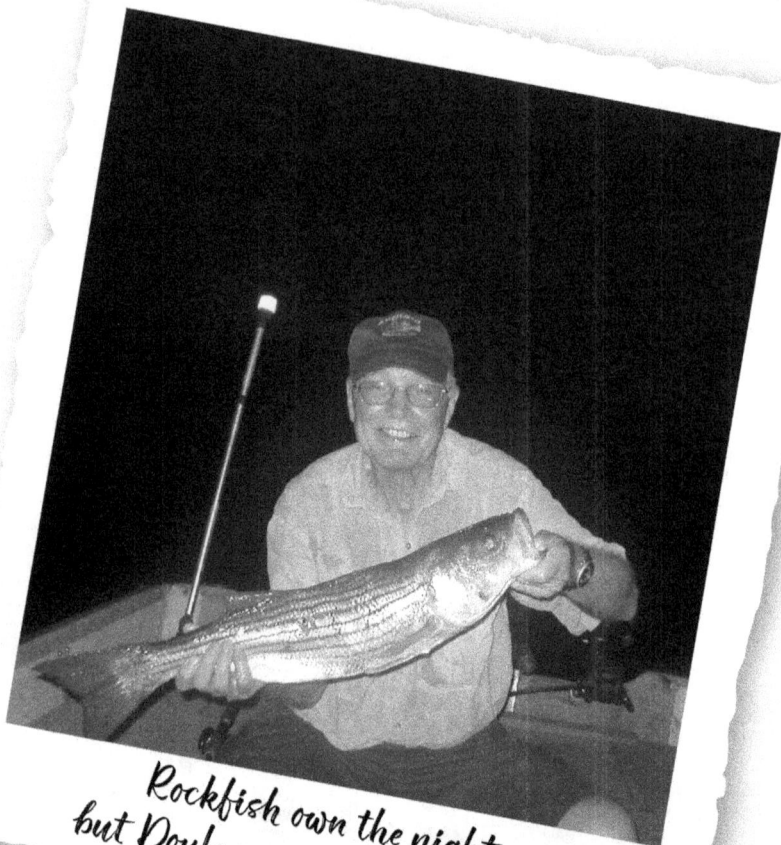

Rockfish own the night,
but Doyle owned this rockfish.

Rockfish Own the Night

TO PLAY WITH THEM, YOU NEED TO KNOW THE RULES

The Chesapeake had at last become quiet. The Bay's summertime revelers—the ski boats, dinner cruisers and jet skis—had long since fled for home. The gulls were finally mute, having settled into their roosts for the night.

As deep darkness descended, I had the Bay to myself.

Snapping out a cast along a well-lit boat pier where I'd seen a swirl in the still waters just a moment ago, I began a studied retrieve, A fish broached the surface behind my plug, but I waited until feeling a solid resistance on the line. Dropping the rod tip and cranking my reel fast, I took up line until it came tight. Then I struck hard.

A fish thrashed noisily out in the nighttime water, my rod tip surged down and my stiff-set drag began to surrender line with a welcome groan. It was going to be a busy night. Game on.

RULES OF THE NIGHT

This time of August, when the sun drops below the horizon, the Chesapeake undergoes a pronounced change. The air is still heavy with the daytime summer heat, so heavy that on a calm evening it makes the languid surface of the Bay's water appear to move like mercury: silver, silent and lazy slow.

But underneath that surface, something else is taking place. With the blazing summertime sun gone, night descending and temperatures finally falling, the Bay's rockfish are wide awake.

Many are moving into the shallows to hunt. They know the baitfish are gathering there in ever-larger schools as they begin the early stages of their fall migration.

Searching about in packs large and small, the stripers are answering to an appetite that has been gradually increasing over the last few weeks. The days are getting shorter, autumn is coming and the nighttime bite is beginning to turn on. The stripers are bolder, even becoming fearless in the dark of these late summer nights. This is a light-tackle paradise and a shallow-water angler's dream.

The angling rewards can be substantial, but fishing the nighttime hours also poses extra dangers. Since the waters are almost always deserted, any assistance an angler in distress may need in case of a breakdown or other boating mishap will be unavailable without a good phone or radio. Can you identify your exact location? In the dark everything becomes extra difficult and confusing. Before you leave home, double check your boat batteries, gas, flashlights, flares and other Coast Guard-required safety equipment. Never venture out unless your craft is in perfect running order.

Always be sure you have an operating marine radio or cell phone, preferably waterproof and submersible. And know how to accurately describe exactly where you are going to be fishing in the event you have to call for help. Let someone know where you are going and when you plan to be back.

Never plan to fish an area in the nighttime that you haven't fished or visited recently during the day. If you don't have a GPS system, be sure to double check the navigational buoys on the way out and note your headings and the numbers on the channel markers.

Things look different in the dark. It can be difficult to find the particular channel or inlet leading to your launch site. It is very easy, however, to get disoriented.

Finally, never venture forth if there is any possibility of storms or squalls, however remote. Check marine weather just before you depart and again while you are fishing. You often can't see bad weather coming in the dark, and summertime thunderstorms can be especially fast moving and violent this time of year on the Chesapeake.

Logan Doyle holds his first fish, a white perch that put his Spider Man spin-cast rod to the test.

A Boy's First Fish

THUS BEGINS A SPORTING LIFE

Having practiced with the colorful rod and reel he got for his fifth birthday, Logan was finally in the bow of my skiff, targeting the water near a rock jetty. He tensed, readied his rod, then sent the small spinner bait sailing through the air.

Though the cast went a little wide, it still landed in a good area. The boy shifted the rod in his hand and cranked the handle. After only a few turns, the reel froze. Concern crossed his face, and he tried to lift his rod tip to help pull in line. But his rod shaft bent perilously down. Then Logan felt the line pull hard. Stumbling a step forward, he recovered his balance just as my eldest, John, grabbed for the back of his son's life jacket. Pandemonium ensued.

The last thing a new angler needs is too much advice, which is exactly what the poor fellow got.

"Pull back, Logan, set the hook! Crank him in, kid, don't let him pull you in the water. Keep back from the gunnel, Logan [as if he knew what a gunnel was]. Rod tip up, rod tip up!" To his credit, Logan was deaf to every bit of well-meaning advice. Chewing determinedly on his lower lip, he leveraged his rod up against the fish's pressure to crank the uncooperative white perch toward the boat.

I have never caught a fish of any kind on a Spiderman spin-cast rod. I hoped Logan would. The model he was using had, at first glance, seemed up to the task. Now it seemed that the power of this fish just might be beyond the outfit's design parameters.

The fish had won the opening rounds, but our intrepid angler refused to give up. After some long moments of struggle and uncertainty, he drew the rowdy perch skiffside. I resisted the impulse to scoop it up at first chance and waited as our young angler subdued the fish properly and led it into the net.

The victory celebration was justifiably over the top, for this was the first fish caught on my skiff by my first grandson, all on his own. I don't think he was any prouder of his conquest than I was of his performance. His dad, my eldest son, was already planning to get Logan his own boat and a half dozen better rods and reels despite his boy's youth.

There were more battles that day, and that evening we dined on the freshest and most delicious white perch fry. The person with the most aggressive appetite for the crunchy tidbits was Logan's younger sister, Isabella, just two years old. I could tell from her appetite, enthusiasm and determination that her older brother had better keep up his fishing skills, because she would be coming strong on his heels. I had already seen to it that she had her own Spiderman and Ice Maiden rod and reel outfits.

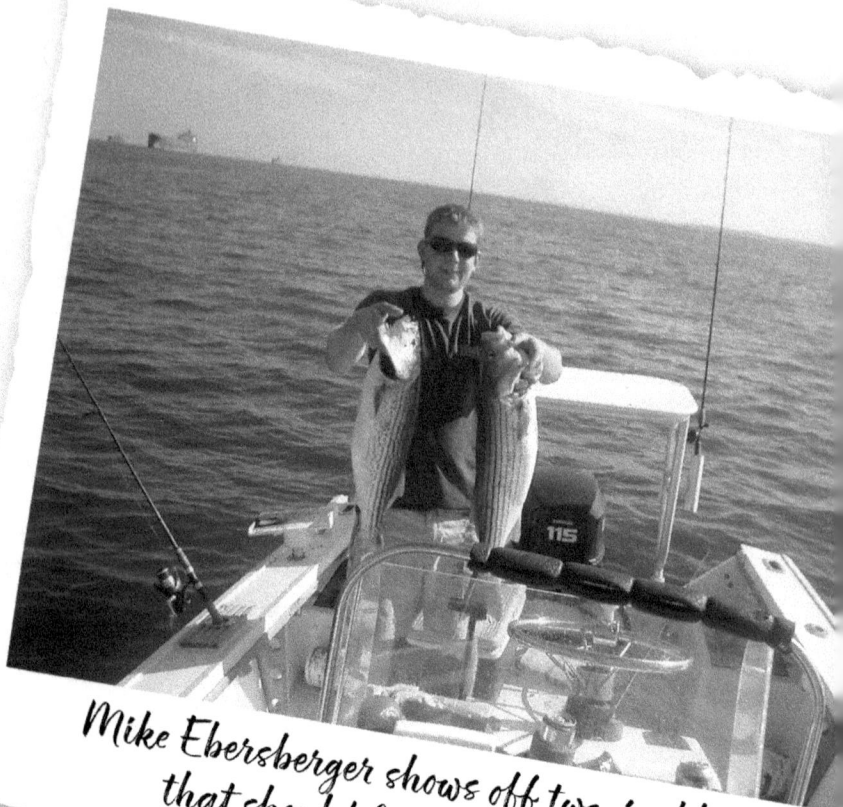

Mike Ebersberger shows off two rockfish that should have known better.

An August Delusion

THE FISH SHOULDN'T HAVE BEEN THERE,
BUT THEY WERE, AND SO WERE WE

It was just after dawn, but we had already been working the shallow cove for almost an hour without a lick of success. Regardless, Mike Ebersberger continued to cast his 5-inch top-water plug from the stern of our anchored skiff with a fierce determination.

Expecting good rockfish on the top of skinny water in August heat was betting against long odds. September is really the earliest month associated with any good surface bite. But even the most remote hope of surface action was enough for us. As anglers, Mike and I are often optimistic to the point of delusion.

"This is it," he said as he threw to the rocky shoreline yet one more time. "I'm going to get one on this cast. I can feel it." I was about to mention how unlikely that appeared just as water erupted under his lure.

A split second later, a sizeable striped bass launched itself into the air, tumbling and shaking, trying to dislodge the lure now fixed in the corner of its mouth. I yelled encouragements to both Mike and the fish.

Most battles with rockfish in the Chesapeake take place in deeper waters. They are invisible struggles, with the fish making short, powerful circling runs, resisting all attempts to bring them up. The striper is largely unseen by an angler until the final moments of the encounter.

But when there is only two feet of water, there are really only two ways for a fish to go, up or long. There is no deep. Visually it can be spectacular.

This fish picked the aerial route. Flinging itself out of the water again and again, it gave us a good look at its five-pound physique. It also planted the horrible and very real fear in Mike that the next head-shaking vault would dislodge his plug.

Mike maintained relentless side pressure on the fish between jumps, first from the right side, then leaning to the left. This confused the striper, finally persuading it to abandon its attempts to fly. It swirled, then darted out of the rocky, snag-filled cove toward the main Bay.

But by then it had exhausted itself, and my partner finally subdued the fish, bringing it to boatside. We had forgotten the net, so I scooped up the handsome rascal with an old bushel basket. Mike was ecstatic. It was his first top-water early fish of the season, and it was August, a very good omen for the fall.

THE SECOND TIME AROUND

Not really expecting much more than one wild stroke of luck that morning, I casually continued to cast my chugger up into the cove. Falling back into an imaginary baitfish-distress scenario that allowed me to induce action to my lure without thinking about it, I worked the plug back. Pop, pause (help, I'm hurt), swim, pause (help, help), swim faster, pop-pop-pop (look out: I'm escaping).

This strike was different. There was no showy geyser, just a heavy surge of water that churned a boil on top the size of a washtub. My rod arced over and line tore out. I was suddenly hooked up with a runaway locomotive.

Over my shoulder I heard Mike mutter, "I can't believe it," as my drag screamed and the fish headed out and out and out. I couldn't believe it, either. Big fish don't show in August. Not in shallow water. My reel was half empty by the time the brute paused. Then it ran a little farther.

It took several long minutes and a lot of effort to work it back toward the boat. Then it took off again. Finally it swirled and showed itself. Still a distance off, we could easily see that it was as big as we imagined, at least a 30-incher.

Mike manned the bushel basket as I drew the beast closer. It was suddenly obvious that the fish was not going to fit. I forgave Mike in advance for its escape. Leaning far over the side of the boat, he sunk our flimsy basket deep in the water.

I led the heavy striper over the rim. Time stopped. Then Mike gave a mighty heave and a loud whoop as the big rockfish and several gallons of water cascaded into the boat. Victory! My first on top water this season and the biggest rockfish I had ever taken on a surface plug in skinny water.

And the action wasn't over. We went on to tangle with a number of fish that morning. None was as big as the 30, but they did range from 22 to 26 inches.

Not bad for a couple of delusional optimists in the heat of August.

Autumn

September

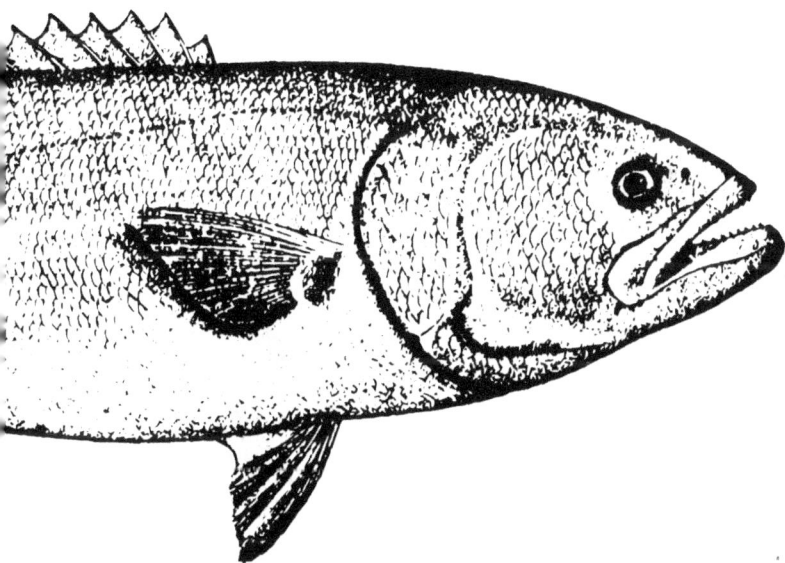

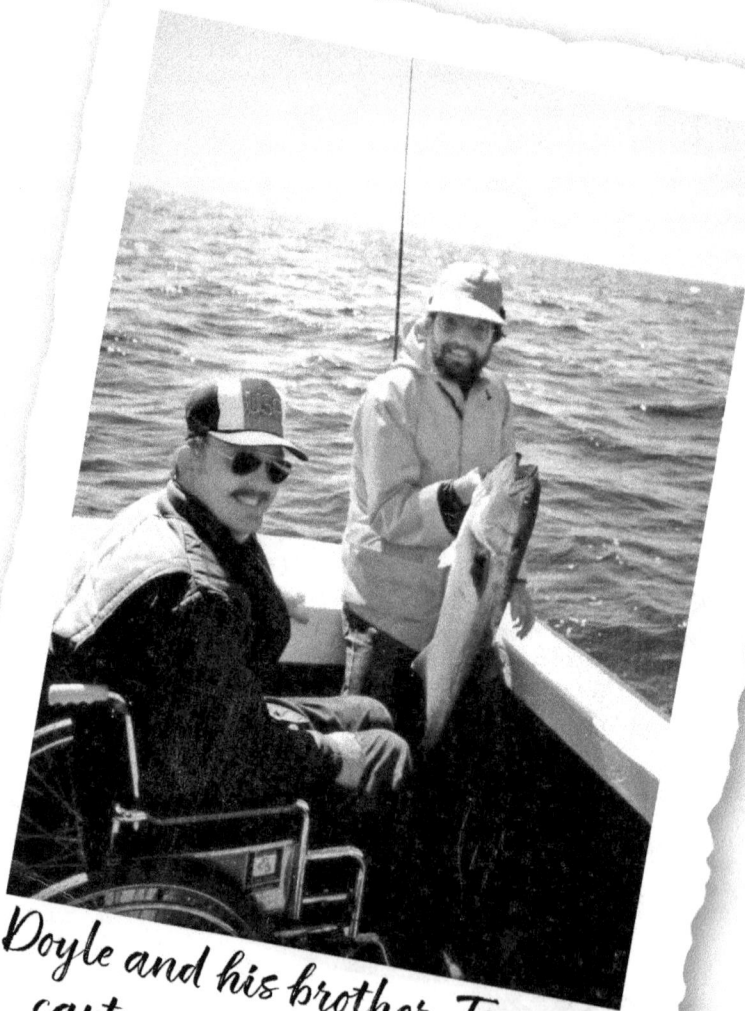

Doyle and his brother Timothy capture a hungry bluefish.

The Season of Hungry Fish

SALTWATER VISITORS ADD TO THE FUN

The autumnal equinox is not yet upon us, but fishing patterns are already changing. September 22 marks the date when the length of day and night are briefly equal, 12 hours each of sunlight and dark.

Because the earth's axis is tilted in relation to the sun, the big bright orb will soon be transiting ever lower on the horizon and our days will be getting shorter, the nights longer. This will bring less of the sun's energy to the northern hemisphere. Thus the chill of fall begins.

Sensing the seasonal changes, stripers are already searching rivers and creeks for baitfish that have begun schooling up and heading downstream toward deeper waters. This autumnal collision of predator and prey prompts the best rockfish fishing of the year.

GETTING IN ON THE CATCH

As the overall bite for rockfish in deeper water has become ever more uncertain, many anglers are pursuing them up into the rivers and creeks and targeting shallow-water structures such as piers, docks, rock groins, jetties and bulkheads. It's often a good idea to focus your search near the mouths of the tributaries, especially along the Eastern Shore.

Throwing soft plastics on light jig heads, anglers are already encountering packs of good-sized stripers searching for bait.

Topwater plugs are flying off sports store shelves these days. The most exciting of all types of light-tackle fishing in the Chesapeake is hooking up with a good-sized striper in shallow water after an explosive surface take.

Cast surface lures to rocky shorelines, jetties and points near the mouths of creeks and tributaries early and late in the day for this action. Poppers such as Chug Bugs, Smack-Its, Atom Plugs and Knuckle Heads will get violent attention. Zara Spooks, Badonk-A-Donks, Sammies and similar prop baits, all walking-type topwater lures, also get their fair share of rockfish (and sometimes bluefish) attacks when the predators don't prefer the noisier poppers.

MEANWHILE, IN THE OPEN BAY

Bluefish and Spanish mackerel are also feeling the approaching changes and feeding more rapaciously. Schools of these fish, as well as hungry stripers crashing equally large gatherings of baitfish in the open Bay, are usually evidenced by flocks of screaming gulls working over the melees. This activity becomes more regular as temperatures drop.

WHAT'S THAT FISH?

In dry years, you'll meet some new players in the Chesapeake. When Bay salinity is very high, encounters with redfish become more frequent. Also known as red drum and puppy drum, reds resemble a croaker with a more pronounced copper hue and one or more large, black spots on their tails. Most of these delicious rascals are undersized and must be released, but there are accounts of bigger fish up to 40 inches. The legal size for a redfish in the Bay is a slot between 18 to 27 inches, and only one per day may be kept.

Small black drum, likewise known as puppy drum, also move into a salty Bay. These fish are a silvery grey and sport bold black vertical stripes that eventually disappear as the fish ages. These young fish are rarer and far more delicious than adult black drum, which are not infrequent visitors to the Bay, all the way up past Baltimore Harbor. Minimum size for a black puppy drum is 16 inches, with a limit of one.

Spotted sea trout are more frequent visitors to our saltier neighborhoods. Similar to the weakfish or gray trout, this beautiful fish sports silvery vermillion flanks with numerous black spots and a yellow canine-fanged mouth. Minimum size is 14 inches, and the possession limit is 10.

In the words of poet Robert Lowell, "Now is the high tide of the year. Fish it while you can."

Jigging around the Bay Bridge, Jamie Avedon nets a good catch.

Secrets of a Jig Master

EFFORT AND THOROUGHNESS CATCH FISH

The northwest wind pushed up some unpleasant seas, forcing us to shift our efforts from the Eastern Shore to the calmer waters on the leeward, western side of the Bay Bridge. That turned out to be good fortune.

That side of the structure abuts Sandy Point State Park and gets a tremendous amount of fishing pressure. Still, by 11 a.m., Jamie Avedon and I had released over a dozen nice stripers and kept three. Jamie did most of the catching as I had my hands full jockeying the skiff around. That had been my plan. My friend had been having great success working a soft jig around the pilings of the bridge supports, and I wanted to observe his technique.

Jamie had armed himself with a 6.5-foot medium-action spin rod and spooled his reel with 15-pound Power Pro braid. Onto the end of the braided line he spliced a 12-to-18-inch section of 20-pound-test fluorocarbon that he then tied to his soft-bodied jig with a Palomar knot.

For lures, we used 5-inch Bass Assassins in the Opening Night pattern: lavender over a clear, soft plastic belly, with half-ounce jig heads with silver glitter. BKD lures (Bass Kandy Delight) and Tsunamis of similar size, weight and color should do as well.

As we methodically worked along the Bay Bridge, I admired Jamie's retrieval style. He would cast his lure out, let it sink (for varied counts), impart sharp, whipping actions, then pause momentarily to let the lure drop, feeling and watching his line to detect any subtle interference during the jig's fall. At the slightest sign of a bump, or hesitation—and sometimes just on instinct—he set the hook.

The violent jigging during the retrieve attracts the fish, but the commitment or strike on the soft-bodied lure usually occurs at the pause, as the bait falls. The bite is difficult to detect as the line tends to slack on the drop. Experience and a deft touch, plus maintaining just the slightest bit of tension with the falling bait, are key.

Also edifying as we fished the bridge were the sequence and targets of his casts. We started from about 40 feet away with Jamie fan-casting around the concrete piers and at varying depths. As we moved in closer, he targeted each component of the support, then between the supports, while continuing to vary the depth of casts.

Next I moved directly into the current, closing on the pier, as he laid his casts up past the structure where he guessed fish might be holding, so that he could retrieve the lure just a little faster than the water was moving toward us.

Finally, I moved the skiff to within 10 feet of the structure, and Jamie flipped his jig directly into and around all of the sweet spots, sometimes called dead-water areas, as I circled the structure. Those sweet spots were typically up-current and down-current of each piling, the areas where a fish can hold with little swimming effort.

That day there was no particular pattern to the hookups. Sometimes the fish were holding off the structure, other times close in or in the middle of the pier legs. Yet other times they were tight in the sweet spots. The only constant seemed to be that it usually took a couple dozen targeted casts before a rockfish hit.

Be persistent, and be patient.

This 25-inch citation-worthy Spanish mackerel taught Ed Robinson a lesson.

Autumn Action

SPANISH MACKEREL MIX WITH BLUES AND ROCK

Ed Robinson had fast-cranked his three-quarter-ounce gold Kastmaster metal spoon back to about 10 feet from our boat when the water exploded high in spray and foam. His drag started screaming, and he could barely hold his rod above the horizontal. When he managed to lift the tip to leverage some line back, it was again jerked down, and the howl emanating from his reel resumed.

We had been chasing flocks of seabirds on Man O' War Shoals just southeast of Baltimore Harbor for almost an hour with our host Dennis Robinson (a retired colonel with the Baltimore County Police Department and no relation to Ed) in his 23-foot center console. Pods of schoolie rockfish to 22 inches were savaging silversides, Bay anchovies and peanut bunker over a large area, and we were cashing in on the action. Flocks of seabirds were everywhere, feeding on live and injured baits. Each group had a small fleet of fishing boats pursuing them and casting lures to the breaking fish.

At first we were sure Ed had a big rockfish on his line. However, the speed of its runs and the sheer violence of the fish's fight soon sowed doubt among us.

"Big bluefish?" someone queried.

"No big blues in the Bay this year," someone else countered.

As Ed finally brought the fish closer, we saw a broad, solid silver flash deep in the water. Definitely no stripes on this beast.

"It's a Spanish," I yelled.

"What's a Spanish?" was the reply.

Then all comment was suspended as Vince Miceli manned the net. The fish went berserk at its sight, and everyone began yelling instructions to Vince, who luckily ignored them while snaring the exhausted fish.

Once it was safely aboard, its sickle-shaped tail drumming the deck, we all admired the catch.

"That devil is a citation for sure," was the next thing out of my mouth. I was familiar with Spanish mackerel and how large they usually run. This was indeed a big one.

Getting the tape out, we marked him at 25 inches, definitely exceeding the citation minimum of 22. It was Ed's first ever Spanish mackerel but not his last of the day by any means. He scored three more.

The Spanish were usually mixed in with rockfish of all sizes, so the day continued in a kind of species-induced tension as each strike potentially could have been a rockfish or a Spanish or a bluefish

The best lures we had thrown initially were soft plastic jigs of the Bass Assassin type, usually 5 inches to 8 inches. The rock were eating them up. However once the Spanish and bluefish made themselves known, most of us switched to silver or gold metal lures as the large cutting teeth of those two species spelled the end of any plastic lure.

A gold Kastmaster in three-quarters to one ounce proved the overall better choice and was as aerodynamic as its name implies. You could easily throw it almost out of sight, a real advantage with the fast-moving, erratic schools we were targeting.

Ed's Spanish mackerel-retrieval tactic (which he attributes to local fishing author Lenny Rudow) was to throw long, let it sink deep, add a five count, then burn it all the way back to the boat.

Surprisingly, the high-speed retrieves with the metal lures proved no handicap to the roaming rockfish that we continued to catch along with the blues and Spanish. It was almost dark when we finally arrived back at the ramp, damp, wrist sore and exhausted.

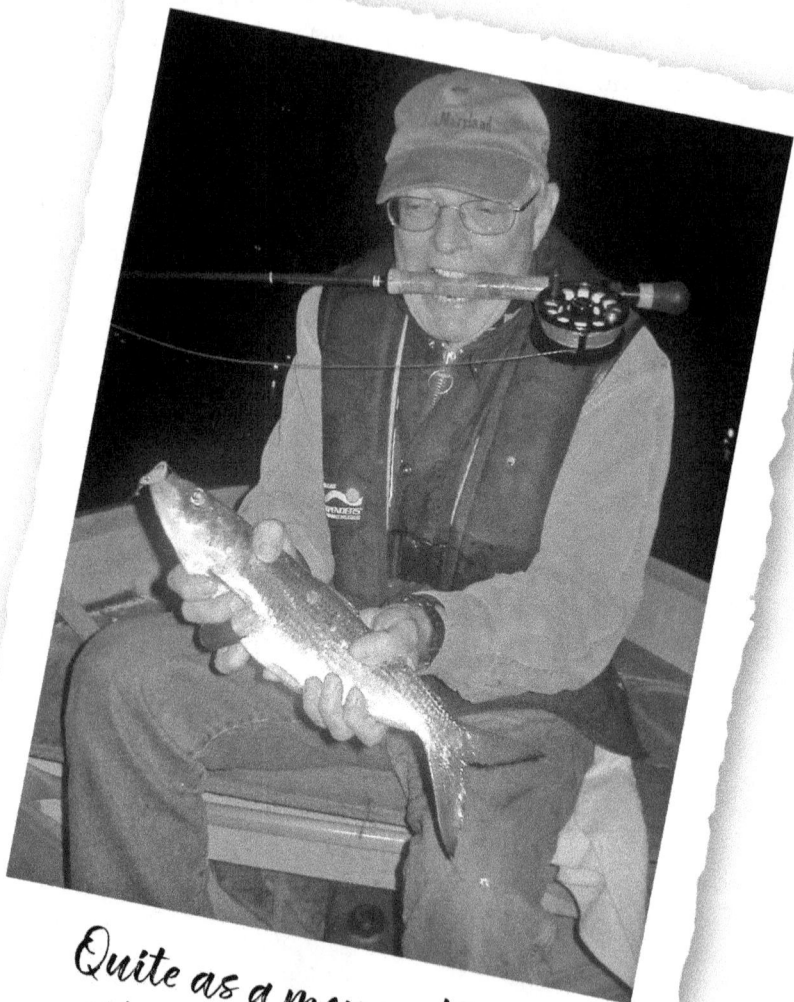

Quite as a mouse, Doyle, with fly rod in this teeth, lured this sound-wary rockfish.

Fish Quietly

THE TRUE MUSIC OF NATURE IS SILENCE

One evening several years ago, when the Chesapeake had experienced a generous influx of gray trout (weakfish), I found a school outside of the mouth of a small tributary south of the Magothy. It was just after dark, the tide was falling and the fish were gathered a long cast away from the inlet to intercept the baitfish, shrimp and small crabs being carried out of the trib by the tidal current.

Throwing a black Clouser Minnow on an 8-weight rod with floating line about 30 degrees off the current direction, I was letting the weighted fly sink and swing across the current along the channel cut. On every third or fourth cast, just as the line straightened below me, the fish would gently take the fly and I would set the hook.

They were nice fish to 23 inches and quite handsome. The fish fights were often extended and uncertain affairs as sea trout are known for their delicate mouth structure. Avoiding putting too much strain on them was a perfect application for the long and supple fly rod.

Anchored close and off one side of the inlet, I was fishing out of a small 14-foot aluminum skiff that I had modified with flush fore and aft deck areas suitable for fly casting. It was a handy little boat with one drawback: Its thin metal hull could be noisy.

I was being very careful moving about, and if I did inadvertently make a noise, I would wait long minutes before resuming any activity to allay fishy concerns that may have arisen. It was a lovely, calm night, and the waters were extremely flat.

During that particular evening it was so quiet I could just make out the distant croaking sound that the sea trout—members of the drum family—often make underwater when feeding in schools. I had been releasing the fish, until I decided to keep one for a meal.

Bringing a particularly heavy specimen on board, I rapped it between the eyes with the weighty end of an aluminum flashlight. It quivered and stiffened. Assured it was sufficiently stunned, I slid it into the ice in my cooler.

Giving the night a few minutes to settle, I once again took my place on the stern casting deck. I had just missed a strike on my last cast when a violent thumping and rattling broke out from amidships. Apparently my sea trout had regained consciousness and was expressing extreme displeasure at its situation.

The sound in the still of that evening was loud and raucous, and despite the fact that I waited a number of long minutes after the noise subsided before resuming my casting, the bite was over and done. The school of fish had fled the area and did not return that night.

The lesson of that evening often comes into mind as I'm fishing. Fish have acute hearing and depend on it to keep them safe. Sound beneath the waves travels five times faster than it does above. Being a thousand times denser than air, water is also an ideal medium for propagation. Sound travels farther, much farther, underwater than above. And fish hear it all, clearly.

The Chesapeake's excellent angling makes it easy to forget that noise discipline is an important factor in fishing success.

Sure anglers catch fish with their engines running, rock and roll blasting on the radio and themselves loudly exuberant. But the smarter, bigger fish have most likely already vacated the area. That's a fact to keep in mind.

A Murder of Crows

The distant screaming of a large group of crows in the trees on the opposite shore alerted me to a serious conflict. Many birds were involved in the skirmish. The apparent violence of their activity gave immediate proof to the collective term for any group or flock of them, "a murder of crows."

Though their noisy confrontations are rarely fatal, there was a definite battle going on that day near the river, of a size and intensity I hadn't seen in many years. There seemed to be an audible majority of American crows in the melee, and as I scanned the tree tops a group of a half dozen of the dark avians broke out and flew directly over me, confirming my suspicions. The lead bird was missing a few flight feathers and was frantically trying to outdistance its five pursuers.

Though the birds were, visually, almost identical, those giving chase were calling angrily in a distinctive accent. It was obvious to my ears that the aggressors were of the common or American crow species and they were harassing a single unfortunate fish crow, which steadily maintained its urgent flight to safety.

The fish crow is a particularly misunderstood bird mainly because most people don't even realize that the unique species exists. Indistinguishable in appearance from the American crow, the fish crow is a separate genus and is quite numerous in this region.

The two crows differ from each other in body size, the fish crow being slightly smaller, and in feeding characteristics, the fish crow preferring to forage for seafood bits along shorelines.

The larger American crow is more omnivorous and aggressive and its population more numerous. The only reliable way to differentiate the two species, however, is by their call sound. The *caw caw caw* of the American crow is clearer and crisper than the fish crow, which has a more nasal quality or burr to its voice, almost a Scottish accent.

Since in some ways I'm, at least subliminally, a bit of a fish crow myself, I've a preference for their company. Their unique caws have always found a friendly echo in my ears.

Since that violent clash, the shorelines have remained curiously silent of both species. I can only hope that the home team retained its grip on our neighborhood. We'll soon see.

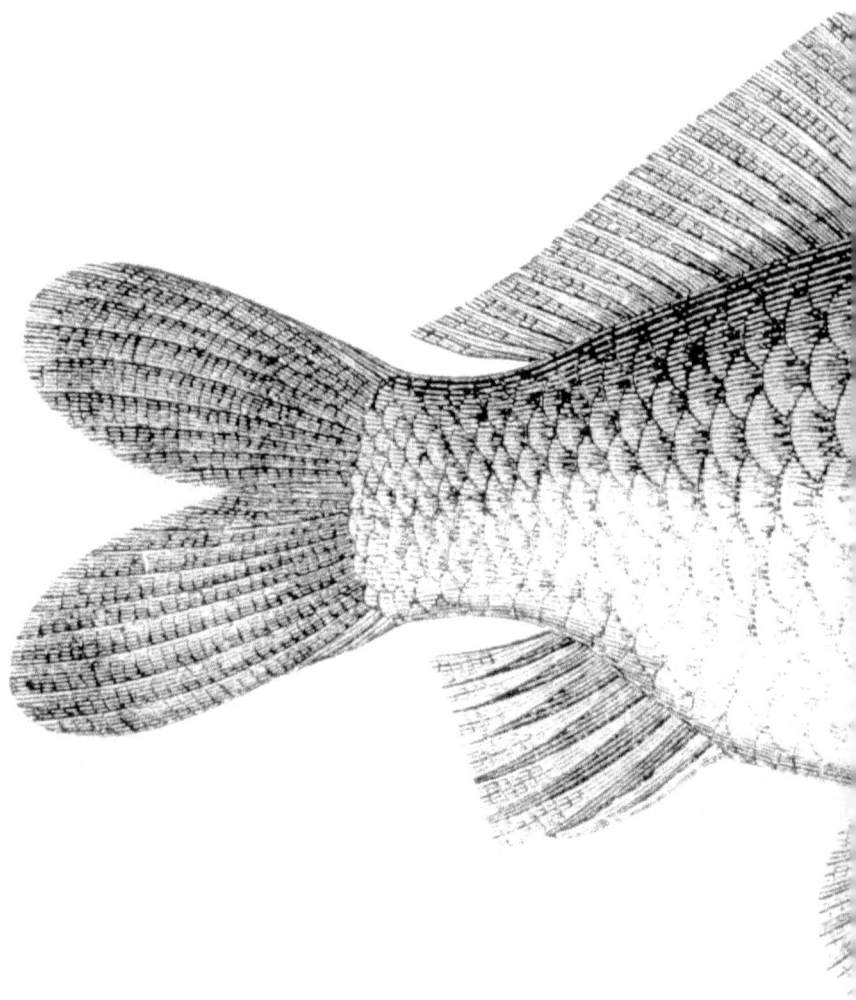

October

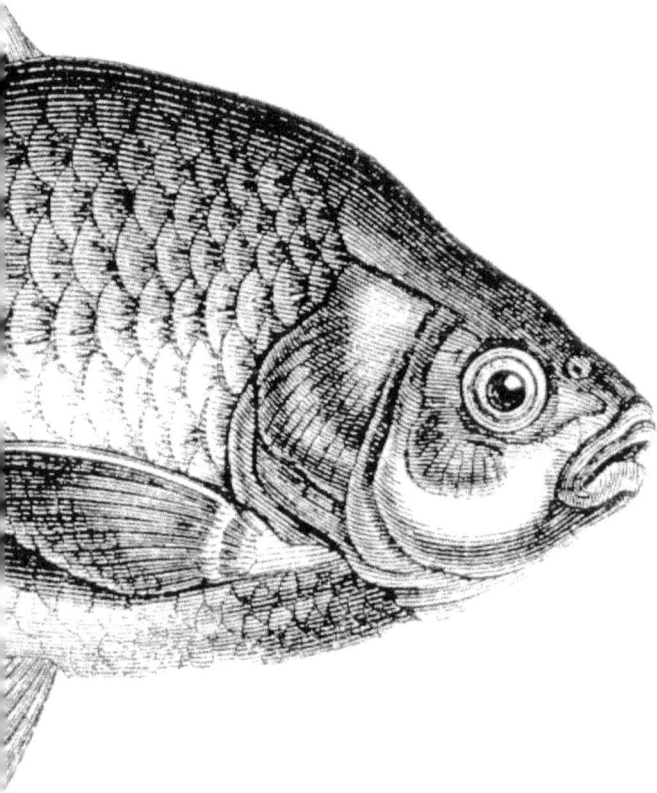

AUTUMN

Wolfie Maines caught a bluefish about his size, but with sharper teeth.

The Piranha of Chesapeake Bay

WHEN SEEKING BLUEFISH, BRING LOTS OF LURES

There is no doubt that a bluefish sees the angler; there is also no doubt that it is just waiting to get in a bite on your fingers.

The perch hit my spinner bait well out at the end of the cast. I suspected it was a good-sized fish because it just stopped when it felt the hook. Finally, as I applied more and more pressure with my ultra-light rod, it moved off laterally and began a determined deeper water run. Then suddenly it accelerated, surged twice in still more powerful lunges—and the line went dead.

As I reeled in, my bent rod still indicated some resistance. Thinking the fish had fouled some debris as it gave me the slip, I paid little attention until my line neared the boat.

Lifting it out of the water, I saw that only the head of my perch remained. Behind the gills were two cleanly cut arcs where its chunky body had been. Bluefish, the piranha of the Bay, had been at work.

Quickly I put down the spinning rod and grabbed my medium-weight plug rod. Selecting a silver-sided, three quarter-ounce Rat-L-Trap and clipping it on, I thumbed the spoon and sent the glittering bait far out over deeper water where the dirty work had just been done. First letting it sink for a slow five count, I began the retrieve. Cranking like mad, I brought the lure back, sweeping my rod to the side for extra speed. It took only a moment to get results. My rod bent over double, and line poured out against the drag. Fish on!

Water broke out at the end of my line as a bluefish, furious at the double-cross, surfaced, changed directions and began another run. It took longer than I anticipated to bring in the four pounder. A blue will invariably surprise you with its power and tenacity. They are one of the strongest fish in the sea.

After netting the flashing, blue-green backed speedster, I sought my long-nosed pliers. Even as I brought the net over the side, the fish's evil incisors flashed as they ground away at the now-scarred surface of the lure.

Carefully grasping the fish behind the head, I removed the hooks as the fish glared at me, still savaging the plug. There is no doubt that a bluefish sees the angler; there is also no doubt that it is just waiting to get in a bite on your fingers.

Adding to the menace of its razor-sharp dentures is the lore that they are coated with an anti-coagulant. Whether or not that is true, one thing I can guarantee: If they do bite, you will bleed profusely.

I gave my aquatic Pac-Man a good tap on the noggin to quiet it as I pushed it down deep in the ice. Keeping bluefish extra cold and cleaning them promptly are two secrets to maintaining their table quality. Fresh bluefish, grilled, broiled or pan-fried the same day it's caught, is as tasty as good seafood gets.

THEY EARN THEIR NICKNAMES

Bluefish come in many size categories: slammers, fish weighing over 10 pounds and up to 30; choppers, fish from five to 10 pounds; snappers, weighing one to five; and tailors, those under a pound. Once you've caught a couple, there will be no question of how they came by those size monikers.

The fish swim in fast-moving schools, never hesitating in one place for long as they seek schools of baitfish. They often eat until fully gorged, then purge themselves and begin again. Seabirds in particular like this aspect and will follow bluefish schools in great numbers, wheeling over them to pick up the copious fish scraps.

In fishing for blues, any flashing lure moved quickly will draw their attention. Steel leaders are usually necessary to protect against their savage bite. Even then, you will lose many fish to competing blues who will bite anything they see around the hooked fish, including swivels and parts of a lure protruding from the struggling fish's mouth.

Larger bluefish have a hard, abrasive surface on the leading edge of their forked tails. When a hooked fish sprints through a dense school of its brethren, any line that contacts another fish's tail will likely be parted. When seeking bluefish, bring lots of lures.

fry_my_best/Shutterstock

Bigger Birds, Bigger Fish

FINDING FEEDING SEABIRDS WILL SAVE YOU TIME AND SPEED UP YOUR CATCH

The seabirds, scores of them about 100 yards away, were wheeling, screaming and diving. We could see the splashes of fish wildly feeding just under the surface. They were not the explosive strikes of the big stripers we had hoped for, but it was impossible to ignore them.

Running ahead but well outside of the feeding school, I chopped the skiff's throttle, turned and eased within casting range. My partner and I flung our lures just to the edge of the action. I was fishing a half-ounce Bass Assassin, and Moe, a half-ounce gold Red Eye Shad.

Moe's rod dipped down almost immediately from a strike, and I felt a sharp tap, tap, tap. "Bluefish," I snorted, "small ones." I could imagine the toothy little devils reducing my 5-inch soft bait to a stub.

My friend landed, then carefully unhooked a wriggling nine-inch snapper blue from the treble hooks of his crank bait and released it. I pulled the shredded remains of the soft plastic body from my jig head and searched in my box for another to replace it.

"This is not going to get any better," I said, looking across the acre or so of small splashes. "Let's vamoose."

Putting the boat up on plane and scanning the horizon, I soon saw another group of working birds about a quarter-mile away.

"Those are big gulls over there," I said. "Maybe we're in luck." Ten minutes later we had two fat rockfish thumping on the deck, though neither was a keeper. A few more casts and a look at the fish-finder confirmed the absence of anything approaching the 20-inch minimum, so off we went again. Across the Bay and into the distance were several groups of birds working above feeding fish. I was glad that I had remembered to top off the gas that morning.

Late August is the beginning of fishing for breaking rockfish under birds. A more exciting fishery just does not exist on the Chesapeake. It's a spectacle of many parts: actively feeding fish, screaming sea birds and—at best—anglers trying to control fish hooked on light tackle and streaking to every point on the compass.

HOW TO CATCH THEM

You can do a couple of things to make the most of these opportunities. First, you need a good pair of binoculars; Models with image stabilizing are particularly helpful. Scanning the waters to find birds that have located the feeding fish will save you a good bit of time.

Next, know your birds. Terns and young laughing gulls are the smaller birds you see wheeling about the Bay. They feed almost exclusively on silversides and anchovies. Bigger predator fish will sometimes key on the small baitfish, but this time of year these schools attract mostly smaller rockfish and bluefish.

Mature laughing gulls are a bit larger, the ring-billed gull larger still, then the herring gull on up to the black-backed gull, the largest of all. When these bigger birds are on the feed, you can bet that the baitfish will be bigger and the game fish chasing them larger as well.

The very best trophy fish-finders are pelicans and gannets. With wing-spreads of more than six feet, they'll be working over the schools of the largest menhaden and consequently the heaviest rockfish, bluefish and Spanish mackerel.

There are other protocols. Never run into the midst of a breaking school. That will put them down and anger anyone else trying to fish them. Turn off your engine while engaging breakers for the same reason, and don't cast into their midst. You'll avoid cutoffs from sharp gill plates of rockfish and teeth and abrasive tails of bluefish if you always work the edges.

If the feeding fish on top are small, go deep. Bigger fish are sometimes on the bottom picking up baitfish injured by the frantic, smaller fish feeding on top.

Squash your hook barbs if you're doing a lot of catch and release. It will make things easier for you and the fish.

We never encountered the big ones that day. We did, however, enjoy lots of hook-ups and releases. And I knew from past experience catching 5-to-7-pound fish that I'd be lucky again another day.

Jigging is a deadly technique
that's simple to master.

Two's a Party

VERTICAL JIGGING SNARES MANY A PAIR

We were drifting my skiff a little bit south of one of the Bay Bridge rock piles in 30 feet of water. I had just lowered my rod tip to let the flashing lure at the end of my line flutter down to the bottom.

We were vertical jigging for white perch, yo-yoing our lures only about 18 inches up and down just off the oyster beds that carpeted the bottom below. On the last jig, when the weight of my lure reaching the end of its fall didn't immediately transmit up my line, I yanked my rod upward in a quick strike.

There was immediate resistance. My rod tip bowed, slightly at first, then arcing over firmly. My drag started to give up a bit of line. I could feel a good fish surging in a tight circle deep below. I guessed it was another fat 11-incher.

I was using a short, 6-foot, medium-power graphite rod with 10-pound Power Pro braid spooled on its small, low-profile, bait-casting reel. It's my favorite rig for October, when the perch are at their table-quality best. Thick, fat and firm, they move into large deep-water schools in the chilling waters of autumn and enthusiastically feed up for the long winter ahead.

The rod I was using was light enough for me to feel every bit of the spirited fight those spunky fish provide. The fast-action stick also had the spine to handle the jigs it took to get down to where the schools of perch were cruising.

At that moment, the tidal currents were gentle, and the thin diameter of the Spectra Braid line allowed me to reach bottom with a light, three-quarter-ounce chartreuse metal Tsunami jig as the bottom lure and a small, size-four white streamer fly about a foot higher up. The big perch usually loved both of them.

Suddenly the rod, arcing much harder, was almost pulled out of my hands. I had to point it down toward the water to transfer the stress more directly to the reel; otherwise, I risked breaking the rod. Line peeled out into the Bay's depth.

My guess was that a marauding striper, attracted by the struggling perch, had hit the second lure on my leader. I had my hands full with an unexpectedly fierce and prolonged battle.

Finally netting a flashing silver five-pound rockfish, I was only slightly disappointed to see that the big perch that had started the melee had shed the hook in the touch-and-go struggle. But that is the luck of the draw when you're vertical jigging.

MASTERING THE ART

Targeting one species won't preclude a second species of fish from homing in on the action. I have caught 8-inch white perch on a 2-ounce, 4-inch feathered rockfish jig, as well as hefty stripers the small, 2-inch dropper flies I favor for white perch. Sometimes a bluefish will jump on, and if its sharp teeth don't snip of the lure it has bitten, you can welcome the blue into the cooler as well.

Sea trout, when they are around, are particular suckers for the vertical jigging technique. Flounder can surprise you as well by attacking your lures when you least expect it, which of course is just about any time you catch one in the mid-Bay.

I heartily recommend that you try vertical jigging. Drifting and fishing straight down beside the boat is a deadly technique and simple to master.

The most difficult part is keeping just the lightest contact with your lure on the drop side of the jigging motion. Fish are most apt to strike as the lure falls toward the bottom. If you feel just the slightest bump—or the opposite, a sudden absence of weight—you probably have a fish on. Strike quickly or it will be gone.

A good electronic fish-finder is the one critical key to consistent success with this technique, if only to eliminate working empty water. While you may not always be able to get the fish that you find on your sonar screen to bite, you will never catch the fish that are not there.

Maurice Klein is taking this
rockfish home for the freezer.

Rocktober

TIME TO FILL YOUR FREEZER

Long before the Colorado Rockies baseball team trademarked the term Rocktober, Chesapeake anglers used the clever moniker to describe the final rockfish feeding frenzy on the Bay. Rocktober is prime time to put some fish in the freezer for the long winter ahead.

In years past, I have been disappointed with fish frozen for longer than one or two months. Fish frozen longer often result in strong-tasting and stronger-smelling dinner. Then I bought a vacuum packing machine. I have since found that vacuum packing makes all the difference.

Allowing any air to reach the fish during storage is a sure way to ruin its table quality. Vacuum packing machines do a better job than hand packing at eliminating all air from the package. Contemporary plastic bags also seem more durable and puncture proof.

First and foremost to ensure best quality is prompt processing. Same day catch and cleaning is essential. The first step after catching is immersing the whole fish in ice (but not ice water).

To prepare a whole fish for freezing, it should be thoroughly scaled, eviscerated and the gills and all traces of organs removed. This includes scraping the backbone and inside of the back of the head of all dark meat. Dark flesh has a gamier flavor and that flavor can migrate to the rest of the meat. The dark section is also where toxins tend to concentrate.

The fish should then be thoroughly rinsed and dried. Finally, rub it inside and out with olive oil. The coating of oil further protects the fish from air and allows it to slide into the vacuum bags without difficulty.

Be careful to prevent the many sharp spines of the whole fish's fins from puncturing the plastic bag during processing and storage. If the fish is moved in the freezer while other foods are added or accessed, it should be re-examined for vacuum failure.

Mark each package as to species and time of harvest. Indelible soft-tip pens are fine for the job.

Finally, vacuum pack and store each fish individually in the freezer—not stacked together—to minimize freezing time.

Freezing rockfish fillets is even simpler. Again, ice the fish immediately on catching. Fillet and skin as soon as possible. Remove the dark lateral line by incising along each side at a sharp angle, pulling that meat away and discarding.

Using the vacuum packer as before, process the flat fillets in quantities that are convenient to use all at once. Mark and freeze as you would a whole fish.

Without a vacuum machine, fillets can be frozen almost as effectively by placing the pieces in appropriately sized heavy-duty zipper-locking freezer bags and adding water. Wrap the bags tightly against the fish, forcing out the air and as much water as possible, seal and place individually in the freezer. The added water ensures that no air will reach the fish during storage.

Maintaining a cold—at least zero-degree—freezer is also essential to long-term storage. Above that, bacteria can emerge and eventually cause unwanted flavor changes. Commercial fish storage is generally maintained at minus-20 degrees, but household fridge may not be able to reach so low a temperature. Use an aftermarket temperature gauge and the lowest possible freezer setting for best results.

I routinely can keep vacuum-packaged whole and filleted fish for a year and water-filled frozen fish up to six months without risking disappointment.

If the integrity of any package is compromised, there are only two remedies: Thaw and cook the fish immediately, or repackage it. Repairing bags with tape or glue does not work.

DON'T STOP WITH ROCK

Rockfish is not the only species that freezes well for wintertime enjoyment. White perch, the premier table fish of the Chesapeake, are also very good for freezing and retaining their freshness when handled properly.

Proper handling means catching, processing and freezing on the same day. Filleted perch can be packaged in units of six to eight fish for dinner for two people with good appetites. If fish on the bone are preferred, scale the perch, cut off the head and eviscerate. Then run your blade down the length of the dorsal and anal fins. Grasping the end of the fin section and twisting will remove those sources of excessive fish bones.

Scatter your packs of fish loosely around your freezer for quick freezing before reorganizing them in one place.

No attempt at preserving bluefish by freezing has ever ended well for me. Norfolk spot, croaker and Spanish mackerel also do not fare well in the freezer.

Though there is nothing like the gustatory experience of dining on fish fresh from the Bay, it's going to be a long, hard winter. A properly frozen Chesapeake fish dinner can be just the thing to chase the cold-weather blues away.

Randy Steck saved the old gang from a skunk.

The Over-the-Hill Gang

THE COMPANIONSHIP OF FISHING ENDURES
EVEN WHEN THE FISH DON'T

One of the rod tips in the stern holders bounced a bit, then again, then bent down deeply. The severe deflection was caused by a hefty rockfish attempting to flee the area with a 7/0 circle hook in a corner of its jaw. Since the sound of the line-out clicker was just under the threshold of our damaged hearing, the striper got a good head start on its escape before anyone noticed.

Years ago, the three of us were members of the self-proclaimed Wild Bunch, with nothing beyond our ken or abilities. A few years later, we reluctantly became an operating branch of The Professionals, skilled but somewhat constrained by age and energy. Eventually, even more years later and deeply into our 60s, we ended up as reluctant participants of the Over-the-Hill Gang. Father Time had gathered us all.

My younger brother Bill; Randy Steck, our adopted brother; and I were lounging in my 17-foot skiff and rocking at anchor a half mile out in the Chester River. It was as adventurous an outing as we managed these days.

Setting up the second of two chum bags, I was hoping for big rockfish. The red-hot bite at the Bay Bridge was mostly spent, and we were chasing rumors of a possible school of good-sized stripers in 20-plus feet of water well out from Love Point off the Eastern Shore.

Sinking one chum bag deep, just off the bottom, and the second streaming at the surface over our stern, I was doing everything I could think of to precipitate some encounters. We were fishing fresh-cut menhaden deep on two-ounce sinkers. Several boats around us were already set up and chumming with two or three trolling through the area. But most of the crews were sitting listless, and we saw no nets being waved.

Randy, with his usual luck, was sitting the closest to the bending rod. Alerted by a number of loud and profane instructions, he finally turned, wrestled it from the holder and began the battle. The fish did not intend to come quietly.

It was a good-sized striper, and demonstrating grace under pressure, Randy eventually finessed it into the net as we all breathed a sigh of relief. The skunk was out and we had a nice fish of about 27 inches in the box. Quickly rebaiting the hook, I cast the rig back out, and we awaited the continuation of action without result. One by one, the boats anchored around us departed for better prospects, while we argued among ourselves whether to wait out the tide, which seemed to have stalled, or to join in the search for better conditions. Eventually we were the only boat remaining. Finally, we decided to move.

But as we brought in our lines, one rod turned out to have a good fish hooked up. Surprised, we endeavored to get this fish to the net. Any rockfish, regardless of how it is seduced, is a good experience.

Remarkably the bite continued to heat up as we then scored one fish after another. Though there were a number of throwbacks (anything under 20 inches for us), our six-fish limit was filled within the hour, just as our bait ran out. It was scarcely 11 a.m.

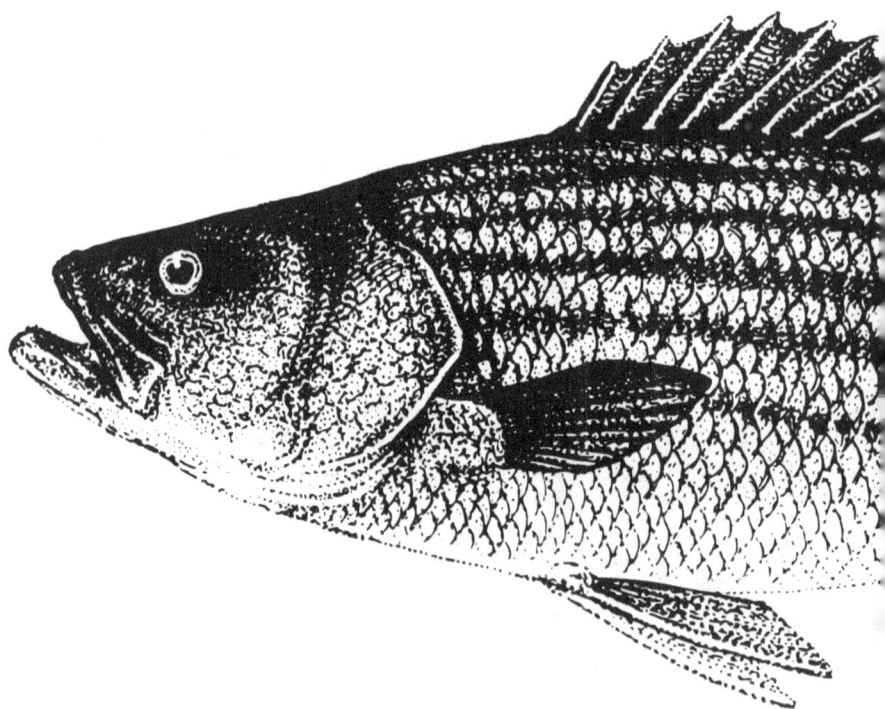

November

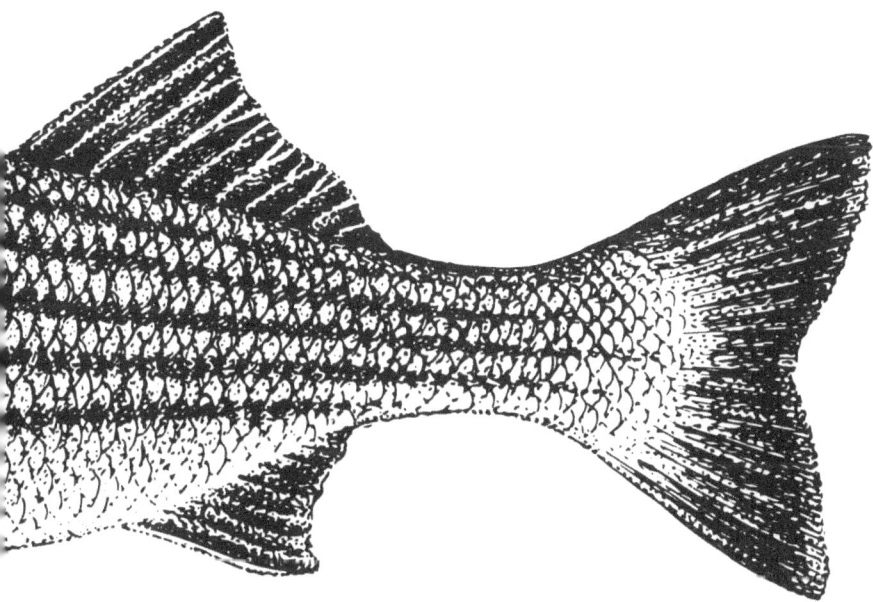

Doyle dressed for cold-weather fishing to capture this rockfish.

The Two Sides of Cold Weather

THE FISHING IS GREAT;
THE DANGERS OF HYPOTHERMIA GRAVE

Finally I had to face it. With morning temperatures in the low 50s, socks were a necessity. With regret, I moved my cargo shorts and warm-weather fishing wear into winter storage last week, removing my insulated long-sleeved undershirts and heavy-weight pants from the closet. Fishing is going to be much more a weather game from here on out.

The good news is that the fishing is getting more exciting. With rockfish and bait fish gathering and feeding up for winter, breaking schools are going to be more and more common. Tossing lures into a cauldron of feeding game fish always provides exciting memories to hold us over unto next spring.

However there is a serious downside to the colder weather, especially on the water. Hypothermia is a medical term that describes the dangerous condition that occurs when your body begins lose heat faster than it can produce it. From lethargy and confusion, eventual unconsciousness and even death can follow.

About 1,000 people in the U.S. die from hypothermia every year.

The very old and the very young are at particular risk of hypothermia, the elderly because their bodies have lost some ability to regenerate and regulate heat, the very young because their small body mass can lose temperature rapidly. Extra care must be taken when they are on the water during cold weather.

During summer months, the spray blowing onto us from a moving boat is a refreshing way to cool off. But in the winter, that experience invites trouble. The body loses heat much faster when it becomes wet, twenty-five times faster when immersed.

A sudden rain squall in October is no longer just inconvenient and uncomfortable. It now becomes dangerous. Worse is falling overboard. Immersion in 45-degree water can result in loss of dexterity and onset of confusion within five minutes, unconsciousness within thirty minutes and death within an hour—if the victim has not drowned first.

Waterproof, windproof and heat-retentive clothing are our primary defenses against hypothermia. Foul-weather coats and pants are not only proof against rain and sleet; they are also protection from the wind and help retain body warmth. Fleece, synthetic insulators and wool are ideal heat retainers. Down should be avoided because once it becomes wet, it loses its insulating qualities.

Don't ignore gloves and footwear. Although our extremities are not critical to our inner core temperature, getting cold hands or feet is extremely uncomfortable. Both neoprene and wool are excellent materials in harsh marine environments. Always wear a warm hat. It is a myth that the body loses 90 percent of its heat through the head—but not if that's your only unclothed area.

Warm beverages give our inner core an extra shot of warmth. Hot cocoa, coffee, tea or plain hot water are effective antidotes to the onset of chill. Avoid or minimize alcohol intake. Alcohol actually promotes body cooling by dilating blood vessels, while giving the illusion of warmth.

Bring extra clothes on board. When a person gets wet, get them immediately into warm, dry clothes. A Mylar or space blanket is an inexpensive, compact and effective item in your cold weather emergency kit. The blanket is waterproof and significantly reduces heat loss.

Once ashore, the quickest way to restore the body's core temperature is a warm (not hot) bath or shower. Avoid exposure to any form of extreme heat. The skin becomes very insensitive during episodes of hypothermia, and burn injuries are much more easily incurred than they would be otherwise.

Cold-weather fishing on the Chesapeake is often fantastic, even better than in more temperate periods. Go prepared for good experiences and great stories. Ignore the accompanying danger at your own peril.

A fat eel iced down to lure a fat rockfish.

Cold-Weather Attractions

A FAT EEL IS THE BEST WINTER BAIT

I could feel my bait swimming strongly downward next to the bridge piling. Judging its descent to a couple of feet off bottom, I thumbed the reel spool lightly, both to keep it out of any rubble it might dive into (a specialty of eels) and to incite my bait's efforts to escape. It briefly struggled against the increased resistance, but that was all that was necessary. Something powerful grabbed the fated critter, then swam steadily away.

A five count allowed about 25 feet of line to slip under my thumb. I slowly raised my rod tip, then lowered it to allow a little slack in the line. Hoping the rockfish had the eel well back in its jaws, I dropped the reel into gear and waited for the line to come tight. When it did, I struck back hard.

My rod bent in a severe arc. I could feel the heavy headshakes of a good fish transmit up the line. Then the striper took off running, headed for the general direction of Baltimore. There was little I could do to stop it. I would just have to wait for it to tire.

THE ART OF EELING

More than any other seasonal change, cold alters fishing tactics and bait for stripers. One of the better tempters, especially for large winter-run stripers, is the eel. Called big rockfish candy because the whoppers love them so much, eel is one of the surest bets for seducing a trophy rockfish this time of year.

The one downside to eeling, as its more dedicated practitioners call it, is handling the slimy devils. Slipperier than a bucket of eels is an old saying. They are impossible to grasp with a bare hand and a challenge to control if you do manage to get hold of one.

Fortunately, there are solutions to these problems. Keeping the snakelike creatures restrained in a net bag in your live-well or an aerated bucket will allow you easy access to them. Using gloves or a piece of rough cloth simplifies holding them until you can manage to get them on a hook.

One of the better alternatives for handling them I've found is to store them on ice. I use a small lunch pail-sized cooler with a good layer of ice (or better yet reusable plastic ice blocks) on the bottom, covered by a thick wet towel. The snakes become dormant when stored this way and will live for quite some time, days even, if maintained cold and covered by another layer of wet towels.

They can be easily handled in this passive condition using just a piece of towel or a cloth glove. Once you've hooked them up and tossed them in the water, they quickly regain their vigor.

Put them on your hook in a way rockfish favor. Because rock have very small teeth, they will usually attack a larger bait toward its head to immediately control it. Your hook should be toward the head of the eel, where the fish is likely to strike.

Sliding the point through the corner of their eye sockets gives the hook a solid purchase. Some anglers prefer to hook them under the chin and out the top of the mouth, particularly if the eels are to be fished weighted on the bottom. Others, especially anglers drifting their eels suspended under release bobbers, hook them lightly under the skin at the back of the head. There is rarely a need to place a second hook farther back on an eel. In fact, using a second hook on this writhing critter will lead to an impossible-to-unravel tangle.

Once a striper strikes, allow it to swim off with the bait. Give it time, at least a five-count, for the striper to subdue the eel and work it back in the throat in preparation to swallowing. Use a strong short-shanked hook, at least a size 4/0, that can withstand a good deal of pressure because your chances of hooking a really big rockfish will never be better.

FAREWELL FISH AND EEL

The rockfish headed toward Baltimore that day probably arrived within not too many minutes. Somehow, during that express-train run, the hook pulled free. I lost the fish, but my hands did not stop shaking for quite a few minutes. It wasn't from the cold.

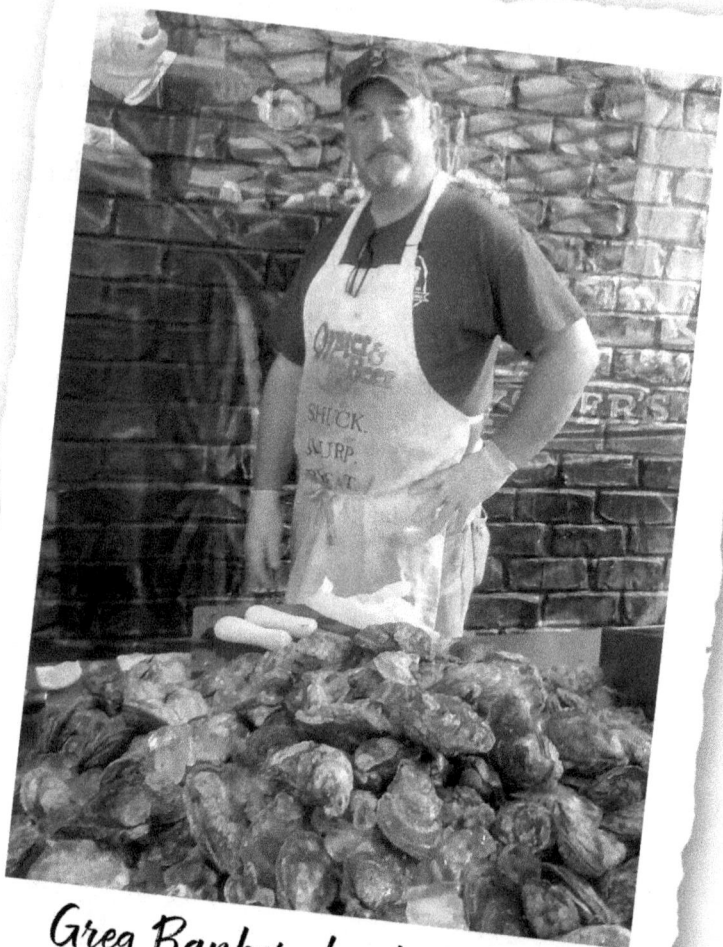

Greg Banker shucks oysters for the Thanksgiving feast.

Enrich Your Thanksgiving Menu with the Bounty of the Chesapeake

FISH, FOWL AND VENISON BLESS OUR YEAR

The tradition of Thanksgiving dinner was first attributed to the Plymouth Bay Colony in what is now Plymouth, Massachusetts. But the practice of a harvest or a thanksgiving dinner was widespread throughout the early colonies and especially around the Chesapeake.

The Chesapeake was by far the richest colony in America in terms of fish, waterfowl and wild game. Capt. John Smith, who first explored the Bay, spoke of being able to "walk across the water" on the bounteous schools of striped bass. Oyster beds were so numerous and large that they threatened the hulls of careless ships. Crabs choked the shallows, waterfowl darkened the skies each fall and wild turkey swarmed the surrounding forests.

In observation of that early American wild game tradition, no Thanksgiving dinner at our house is complete without at least a few of the dishes (or variations thereof) that were sure to have been served around the Bay for 400 years.

CHESAPEAKE OYSTERS

Chesapeake Bay oysters are a treat that never gets old. I have two favorite ways to serve them: On the half-shell with a squeeze of lemon and a dash of Tabasco; and barbecued, smoking hot off the grill, with a seafood cocktail sauce.

There were always wild geese and ducks on Tidewater tables because their migrations were at their peak this time of year. The flights of waterfowl coming down from the north no longer darken the noontime sun as they once did, but there is still a fair flurry of Canada geese, mallards, black ducks, widgeon and teal blessing our shores in autumn.

ROCKFISH CEVICHE

Two rockfish fillets, or other firm,
white fish (about 1½ pounds)
sliced into pieces about 2 by ½ inches.

1T salt

2T olive oil

1.5 large sweet onions, cut in half lengthwise,
then sliced very thinly

2 or 3 large cloves of garlic, minced

1 to 3 jalapeno peppers, chopped

4 lemons

4 limes

1 handful fresh cilantro, chopped: optional

Put fish in a glass bowl. Add all ingredients but citrus, then gently mix. Add freshly squeezed juice of lemon and lime to cover ingredients in the bowl. Gently mix again so that all pieces are exposed to the juices. Cover and refrigerate at least five hours, better yet, overnight.

Taste and adjust spices. Serve drained on a bed of lettuce with a garnish of thinly chopped spring onions plus a side of French or artisan bread or your favorite crackers.

WATERFOWL MEDALLIONS

Grilled teal is a great starter, for these birds are scarcely larger than a pigeon. You can also substitute smaller pieces of larger waterfowl.

Fillet breast meat and, slicing against the grain, cut into medallion-sized pieces about three-quarters inch thick. Marinate overnight in olive oil, rosemary, minced garlic, and salt and pepper.

Wrap each piece generously in thick bacon strips. Then quickly cook over a hot charcoal fire until the bacon is crisp and the duck medium.

Or skip bacon and drop pieces individually into a hot cast-iron skillet and quickly brown both sides. Remove and store in shallow bowl in warm oven.

Deglaze the skillet with one-half stick butter and one-quarter cup brandy. Drizzle over the browned medallions. Garnish with chopped parsley and serve.

CRABMEAT-TOPPED SALAD

Our garden salads at Thanksgiving have a Chesapeake twist, with backfin crabmeat to top everyone's bowl of mixed salad greens sprinkled with mustard vinaigrette.

VENISON QUARTER

Whitetail deer also graced the tables of our Colonial fathers, and while not nearly as plentiful as today, they were still very highly regarded. A hindquarter of young whitetail deer makes a wild Thanksgiving centerpiece.

Rub the roast with coarse-grained salt and puncture thoroughly with a sharp thin knife and insert stout slivers of garlic throughout. Then coat it with olive oil, and pepper and sprinkle with fresh, minced rosemary. Allow the meat to reach room temperature before cooking.

Roast about an hour—until the venison reaches 135 degrees—on a covered charcoal grill with mesquite chips added for a good smoky flavor. Slice the meat thin and across the grain.

FILETS OF ROCKFISH

If you're lucky enough to still be fishing the week of Thanksgiving, fresh rockfish filets add Colonial variety to your holiday spread. I like to keep my rockfish simple. Anoint it with olive oil, salt and pepper, then broil. Flip when the fish begins to brown, and remove when it flakes.

Smother the filets with sliced, briefly sautéed mushrooms and chopped pimentos in a lemon butter sauce.

COLLARD GREENS

Rinse, stem and chop two pounds of greens. Combine in large saucepan two bottles of beer, two tablespoons olive oil, one-half cup chopped country ham and salt and pepper. Add greens and simmer until tender.

Happy Thanksgiving!

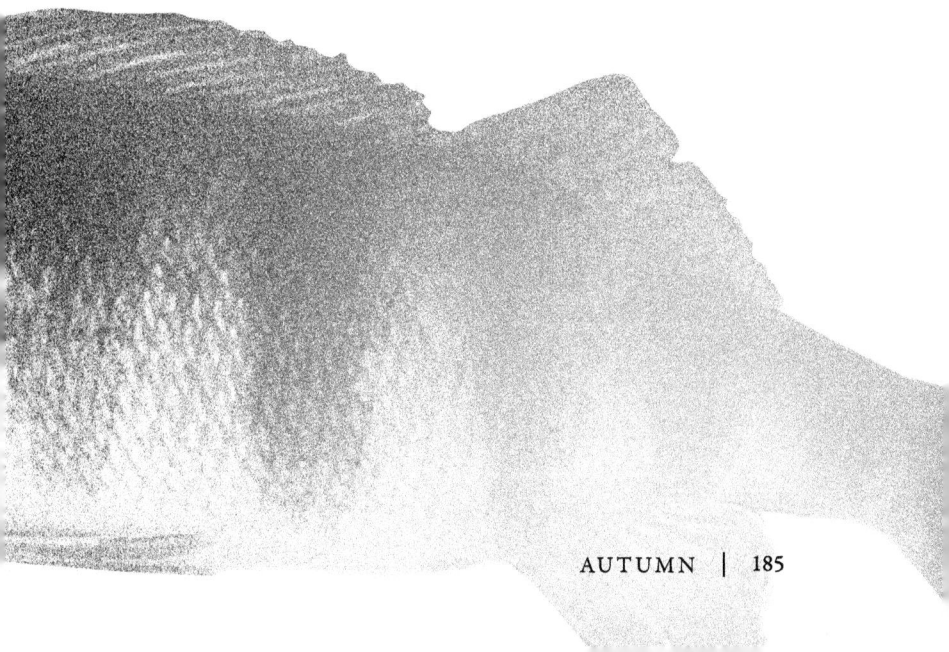

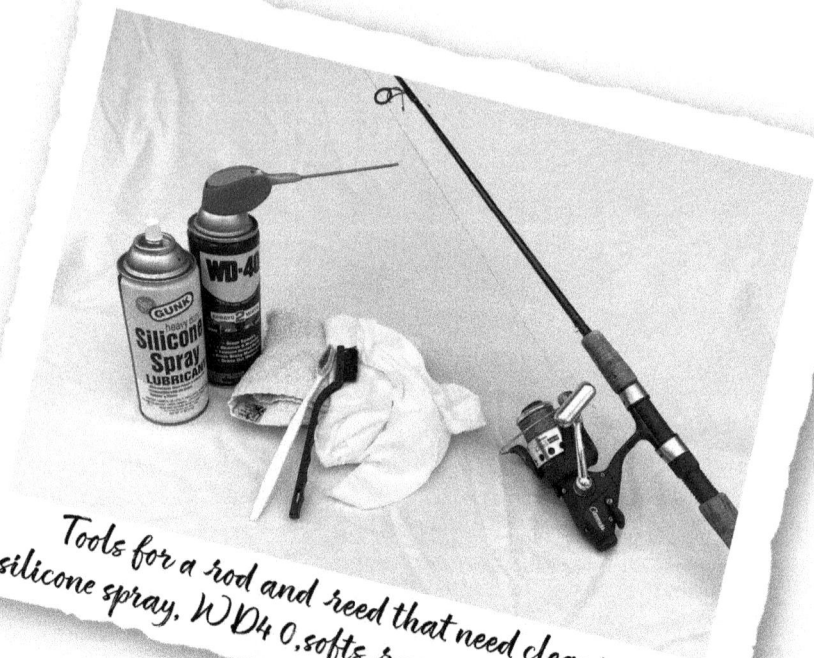

Tools for a rod and reed that need cleaning: silicone spray, WD40, softs rags and a toothbrush.

Taking Care of Business

HOW TO PREPARE YOUR ROD AND REEL
FOR THE LONG WINTER'S SLEEP

November is a cruel month for an angler. Days reminiscent of more temperate times are inevitably followed by extended torrents of icy rain and relentless wind, and we know it will only get worse. But while it's horrible outside, it does provide us opportunity to prepare some of our sorely used equipment for the long winter's sleep.

Salt is the prime enemy, and if equipment has been on the Chesapeake, it has acquired some. Any amount is trouble. Even stainless steel and anodized aluminum are not impervious. The salt will draw in moisture from the air, make a nasty little soup and slowly eat away at virtually any metal it contacts.

Even if you're a sweet-water angler, your equipment deserves a good cleaning before retiring for the season. Common water scum and dirt will degrade tackle.

With proper care, your tackle will certainly last longer and perform well for you next year.

So get a toothbrush, a can of marine-grade silicone spray, WD-40, some soft rags and let's get at those tired rods.

STEP-BY-STEP

Run the length of each rod section under tepid water. Rub with a wet, soapy rag, rinse and dry with a soft towel.

Next, scrub the base of each guide with a brush soaked with WD-40 until there is not a hint of dullness. Stubborn stains or green deposits (sure signs of salt) can be removed by adding toothpaste to the scrub. Rinse and towel off again.

Now, apply the marine silicone lubricant to the entire rod. Let it sit for a few minutes before buffing it with a fresh towel until it looks like new.

If you've got roller guides, make sure the rollers spin. If they don't, you can easily remove them and soak them in WD-40 or any light lubricant until they free up. If they don't free up, replace them. Frozen rollers will wear weak spots in your line while you are trolling.

Take a look at the grips. Foam grips are easily cleaned with a vigorous brushing of soapy water. Cork is more demanding. It is a wonderful material, soft, warm to the touch, durable and a perfect fit for the grip on light-tackle rods. But it is not impervious to weather, and it attracts dirt and fish scum like a magnet.

The first step is to wet the cork down with tepid water. Then take a piece of fine grit (220) wet/dry sandpaper, apply water and a little liquid detergent to it and go over the entire grip. With extreme cases, you can add a little kitchen scouring power to the mix to speed things up. Be especially careful not to scrub the metal reel seat or the rod itself.

Once you are satisfied that you've gotten the grime removed, rinse the entire grip thoroughly, especially the reel-locking mechanisms; you do not want any residual grit trapped there.

When it dries, the cork will look surprisingly close to new. If your cork is bleached out and brittle dry from excessive exposure to weather, apply neatsfoot oil. Wipe the excess off after giving it a few moments to absorb.

Do the WD-40 and toothbrush routine to the reel seat, being careful to reach all areas, especially the reel-seat hoods, locking bands and threads. Towel dry. You can apply a good grease to the threads if you'd like, working it under the locking bands.

Last, if your rods are multi-piece, rub a candle stub over the male ferules. Lightly twist the sections together to distribute some of the wax inside the female unit. Next season, you will find that the wax coating will make assembling the rod far easier, and it will keep the rod sections from coming apart in use. It will also prevent them from sticking together when you are breaking your rod down.

Your rod is now ready for storage. Choose a dry place with even temperatures. Store the rods vertically if possible, or lay flat to prevent a possible set.

This routine may seem tedious, but keeping your gear in top shape will produce many rewards. When springtime comes and your tackle fairly leaps from its place of storage, gleaming and ready for action, you'll be glad you tucked it in so carefully.

Winter

December

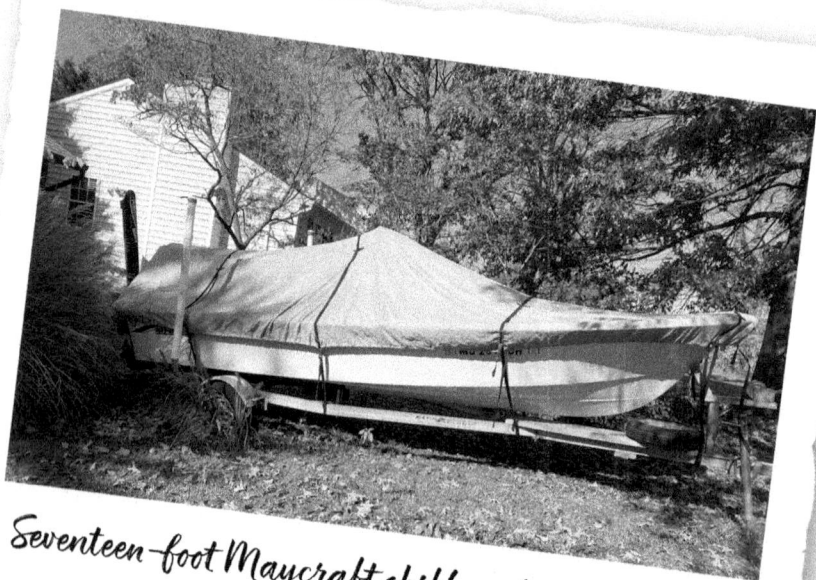

Seventeen-foot Maycraft skiff under winter cover.

Winterize Your Small Craft

A SAD BUT NECESSARY CHORE

Getting the boat ready for winter causes me emotional upheaval. It is not only a burden of hours but also an unwelcome recognition that one of my great avenues to peace and contentment will soon be closed off. I've made my checklist, only to avoid it for weeks. Each item is a step closer to a kind of prison, so I'm not fond of any of the unavoidable tasks facing me. But do them I must.

To cope with my reluctance, I've adopted a gradual wintering schedule over the course of a month of more, prioritizing chores in such a way that any sudden boating reactivation does not set the schedule back to zero.

I start out by thoroughly scrubbing the decks and the interior nooks and crannies with a strong detergent fortified with bleach. If you think getting a deck and interior clean in the fall is difficult, try doing in the spring after the grime and gunk has solidified on the boat for four or five months.

Waxing in the springtime is a necessity, and a winter wax makes just as much sense. The hull needs a film of wax protection from extended cold wind, rain, snow and otherwise brutal weather.

Next is the big salt flush. Belting the flush muffler on my outboard motor's low unit water intakes and coupling it to the garden hose and fresh water is the first step in this necessary process for put-up. Salt never sleeps. That simple substance, if given opportunity, can punish any internal combustion motor.

You dare not allow a deposit somewhere in the inner channels to do its dirty work over the upcoming long and frigid months. I will run the fresh water flush for at least 15 minutes to be sure the motor is warm, all thermostats are open and most salt deposits are gone.

I've flushed the motor periodically during the fishing season, but a thorough cleansing before put-up always makes me feel better. As insurance, I'll hook up a mixing unit adapter to the hose and fill its container with Salt Away, a specialized marine product for heavy-duty salt removal.

Salt Away is non-toxic, biodegradable and safe to use in any environment. Its intense blue color guides the length of the flush. As soon as the container looks like it's almost empty of the blue concentrate, in just a minute or so, I'll stop the flushing so as to ensure some remains in the motor over the winter to continue its salt protection.

The next procedure is the lower unit gear grease. Draining the lower unit is a simple matter; just remove the lowest drain plug near the propeller.

Place a tub or a bucket under it to catch the old lube. Lever the motor near vertical, then remove the plug located higher above the unit to allow it to drain.

Pay close attention to the color of the lube as it drains. It should not be any shade of gray. Black is a sign of a well-used lube. If water has infiltrated through any of the driveshaft seals, the lube will turn gray and indicate that the seals (there are usually two) need to be replaced. Not to do so is to risk your motor's lower unit bearings, driveshaft and the very gearing itself.

Do not wait until next spring to address this problem, especially if you intend to have the work done at a marina.

Winter months are a slack time for the industry, but spring is always bedlam. Starting in early March, it could take many weeks for a mechanic to get the time to do a lower unit while you sit stranded in port.

Replace the lower unit lube by filling it from the bottom vent to the top. When lube begins spilling out of the top plughole, firmly replace that plug. The heavy viscosity of the lube will prevent any draining back out the bottom vent while that plug is being positioned. Use the very best quality lube as this 80-to-90-weight lubricant protects the motor's transmission gears.

Next you'll want to change the motor oil (assuming a four-stroke) and the oil filter. Once again, this is not the place to save money. I recommend only the best synthetics.

I top off all of my motor's grease fittings to ensure there are no internal cavities to attract condensation, then spray down the entire top end under the cowl with WD-40. That product was originally developed to protect NASA rocket parts, so I assume it will defend my outboard.

Since I add fuel stabilizer and an anti-carbon additive to my boat's gasoline supply during winter, I've no need to treat my fuel for the water. If you don't share in this practice, treat all your gas with a ring-free additive and a fuel stabilizer. Run it into your engine thoroughly during the last flushing and prior to putting your rig up.

Completely disconnecting your batteries is one of the last must-dos. Most outboard motors and the boat's accompanying electronics continue to draw at least a small amount of power. Unless each battery is connected to a maintenance charger, it will likely be damaged and have to be replaced in the spring.

Finally, a weatherproof boat cover is a must for maintaining a clean craft.

Hope springs eternal in an angler's heart. I'm always expecting one last good day before winter closes us out. In the meantime, I'm checking off my winterizing list in case the season is really over.

Winter gear:
West Marine foul weather coat; fleece unitard;
Patagonia expedition-weight fleece zip neck;
pull-on rubber bottom lined boots;
wool fingerless gloves; wool hat.

Winter-Adventure Advisory

FREAK WARM DAYS MAY BE TOO GOOD TO BE TRUE

From the front window, I saw the trees about my house were finally still. The sun was shining at last, the forecast was for 60 degrees, and one more day on the water suddenly looked possible. After all, rockfish season was still open.

I had covered my skiff for the winter just days before, but that wasn't a problem. One of the benefits of maintaining a super-simple system is that it would take only minutes to pull the cover off and reconnect my electrics. My fuel and motor had been treated for the winter as well, but I knew from experience that the engine would purr like a kitten as soon as I hit the starter button.

Opening the door to assess the scene more closely, I saw my breath in what I soon discovered was 30-degree air. Another faulty forecast: What a surprise. Retreating into the kitchen for more hot coffee, I pondered my habit of wishful thinking.

A humorous image registered as I considered another event years before when we had a spate of wonderful days of 70-degree weather during an otherwise bitterly cold December. Calling my friend Mike on the third day of the heat wave, I suggested we take advantage. He agreed. From my house we traveled snow-edged streets, towing my now de-wintered skiff festooned with hastily readied fishing rods.

At the nearby ramp expecting a bonus day on the water, we both broke out in laughter. The ramp, the creek and most of the river were still frozen solid. We had forgotten the effects of the previous weeks of near-zero weather. It is amazing what we can convince ourselves is possible from an overwhelming desire for it to be so.

Since then, I have tried to stay safe by making a checklist of critical elements that had to be verified before starting out, no matter how much I, or my companions, desired the adventure. Today's technical achievements have made most of the elements easily determined from the comfort of home by referring to the many monitoring website buoys about the Chesapeake.

The best website to reference is this marine forecast:

NOAA.GOV:
https://www.ndbc.noaa.gov/station_page.
php?station=TPLM2

for current conditions on the water. Thomas Point Light Station (TPLM2), located mid-Bay, gives actual location wind direction, speed, water temp, air temp and some data history so you can discern if conditions are generally improving, consistent or worsening.

If you've got air temps in the high 50s and water temps in the 30s, you can bet that when you're on the water it'll feel a lot colder than the top number suggests.

For my open skiff, I do not entertain cold breezes above 10 knots and generally prefer them less, ideally much less. As to the state of ice, I'm afraid you'll have to rely on your recollection of just how cold it's been recently and remember that the Bay ice is just as slow to melt as it is to form.

You can get more specific location data from a number of other Chesapeake Bay buoys:

https://buoybay.noaa.gov

If you've identified a sheltered shore you want to visit, these sites could give you a real-time picture of just what to expect including wind speed, direction and the temperatures of both that local water and air.

Remember always that fish will be using smell to find their food and moving more slowly, sometimes much more slowly, than in warmer months.

Finally there are the usual cold-weather fishing dictates such as layering with expedition-class clothing, windproof and waterproof coat and pants, extreme weather socks, footwear, hats and gloves.

Get off the water anytime you begin to feel clumsy, chilled or even a touch confused. Those are the signs of incipient hypothermia, and that can be deadly.

Bella, Hobbes and Logan

Versatile, Valiant Labradors

INDOOR AND OUT, ON LAND, WATER AND RUGS,
THESE DOGS ARE UP FOR THE JOB

Labrador retrievers will plunge into frigid waters, swimming any distance to retrieve your downed waterfowl. They'll hurl themselves into thickets of thorny briar to roust clever pheasants. They'll race across acres of knee-deep snow to secure a wing-tipped goose and comb through thick, waist-high fields, foot by foot, to flush out a crafty quail. A dog is truly an outdoorsperson's best friend.

During fishing season, my dog Hobbes is a boon companion on days temperate enough to invite him along. He especially enjoys perch fishing and will protest endlessly when I throw the small fish back until he gets one for himself. Then he will lick it clean, take it forward and carefully chew it up and eat it, head to tail and with never an ill effect.

At home, he's a member of the family. At holiday parties he is especially cooperative with our activities, particularly when children are about. He allows them just about every kind of privilege one can imagine. Hovering about them like a doting uncle, Hobbes will devotedly lick their fingers free of any sticky frostings that might linger to foul the draperies.

The day after Christmas this year, we found our seven-year-old grandson, Logan, after lunch, curled up with our Lab in his small, comfy kennel, both sound asleep. Earlier that day Hobbes patiently sat at four-year old granddaughter Bella's tea party table, set with dolls, cups, saucers, and plates of cookies until he was rewarded with his own small pile of treats.

Most children never pass by him without trailing their fingers through his thick, shiny black fur, and none have to look far for him, as he inevitably follows wherever they've wandered, eventually picking up their discarded socks, hats and gloves and, for some reason, bringing them to me for safekeeping.

Throughout the past holidays, drivers delivering packages to the house were regularly greeted with the most unusually ferocious Lab talk as Hobbes announced that no one would be permitted near the presence of his young charges without thorough screening. Repeat delivery people soon learned to be extra quiet in the discharge of their duties. Hobbes also patiently modeled the various scarves that were wound about his neck to see which was preferable for whatever occasion the kids were imagining or organizing. Hats were often attempted but never successfully accepted for long.

When the busy holidays were finally over and the various houseguests were packing, the most overheard comment was not how much they wanted to remain at Nana's house or the cookies and treats they enjoyed, or the presents, decorations, or fun times. It was how much they were going to miss Hobbes and his warm, furry embraces.

I've enjoyed the company of bird dogs for over 50 years, but Hobbes is my first Labrador. And while I dislike comparing their respective merits (they were all outstanding companions), I have to admit that none attached themselves to the children quite like our Lab. I also just noticed that only since the kids have gone, has he returned to my side again, wherever I go. Labs, apparently, also have a great sense of priority.

Five dressed lures.

Dress Your Lures for Success

THE ART OF ANGLING IS IN THE DETAIL

Wintertime is downtime for most anglers. But in waiting out the bitter weather, you can do a number of things to increase your success in the season to come. One of the best is dressing up your favorite plug, spoon or metal jig.

Dressing a lure means adding feathers, bucktail, synthetic hair or flashy filament to the trailing hook of the bait. Since that hook generally swings free with the action of the lure, dressing magnifies the movement and provokes a second focus for the gamefish and, more importantly, a trigger to their strike response.

Wave a small object in front of a tabby cat, and it immediately becomes interested. Add a brightly colored bunch of feathers or hair (minus the hook, thank you) swinging at the end of that shiny object, and you had better mind your fingers.

Seeing that additional, animated attraction, our gentle tabby launches itself, claws extended, to capture the fascinating tidbit. Rockfish will attack like that as well.

Today, especially in our mid-Bay, with all of the fishing pressure of our area's numerous anglers, showing the fish a lure with a little extra attraction can mean the difference between landing a limit, a lunker or a skunk.

There are two ways to dress up a lure to provide that extra attraction. One is to purchase a dressed hook and use it to replace the bait's trailing treble. Dressed trebles are sold at all sports stores and better mail-order houses.

Google *dressed saltwater treble*, and you will get thousands of hits on sources and information. But beware: Depending on the quality of the hook used, they can be expensive, especially if you have a number of lures you want to improve.

The second way is more interesting and less pricey. Make the dressings yourself on the hooks already on the lure. With minimal equipment, you can create your own dressed treble with your own unique and attractive teaser—and you can do it cheaply.

Tying materials are inexpensive at most of the same stores that handle the dressed trebles or at locations handling fly-tying materials. The feathers, generally listed as saltwater saddle tackle, are available in more colors than you ever thought possible. But white, yellow or chartreuse will always do the job nicely.

Buy them in packages of a quarter-ounce, and you will have enough feathers for a long season and lots of lures. You will also need thread, head cement or clear nail polish (Sally Hansen's Hard As Nails is excellent) and an inexpensive tying bobbin. Danville's Flat Waxed Nylon is a strong, durable and commonly available thread that I recommend for this application. Buy red, white or black.

The tying bobbin holds the thread and makes wrapping on the feathers much simpler. The head cement seals the thread wraps and protects them. All of these items can be had quite inexpensively.

The last thing you need is a hook holder or hook vise. These are available at the same places that provide the hooks, thread and bobbin. Or you can also improvise your own. A pair of vice grip pliers will also do the job, perhaps not as prettily as the custom vise.

STEP BY STEP

Remove the hook from the lure (split-ring pliers can help here). Clamp it in the vise at the hook bend with the hook shack parallel to the ground. Cut two tackle feathers so they are at least twice the length of the hook. Placing them together along the hook shank and using the thread and bobbin, wrap in the feather butts close to the hook's eye so that the tips trail out between two hooks of the treble.

Do that for each of the three gaps. Finish wrapping off the head formed by the thread so that it is compact and even. Then thoroughly apply head cement or nail polish to the wrap, give it two coats and let dry, and you're ready to attach the newly dressed hook onto the lure of choice.

Whatever success you had with this bait in previous seasons will be amplified by the extra attraction this dressing provides. Plus you'll have a bit of your own handiwork at play at little cost and effort. For now, it's a great way to while away a cold winter evening.

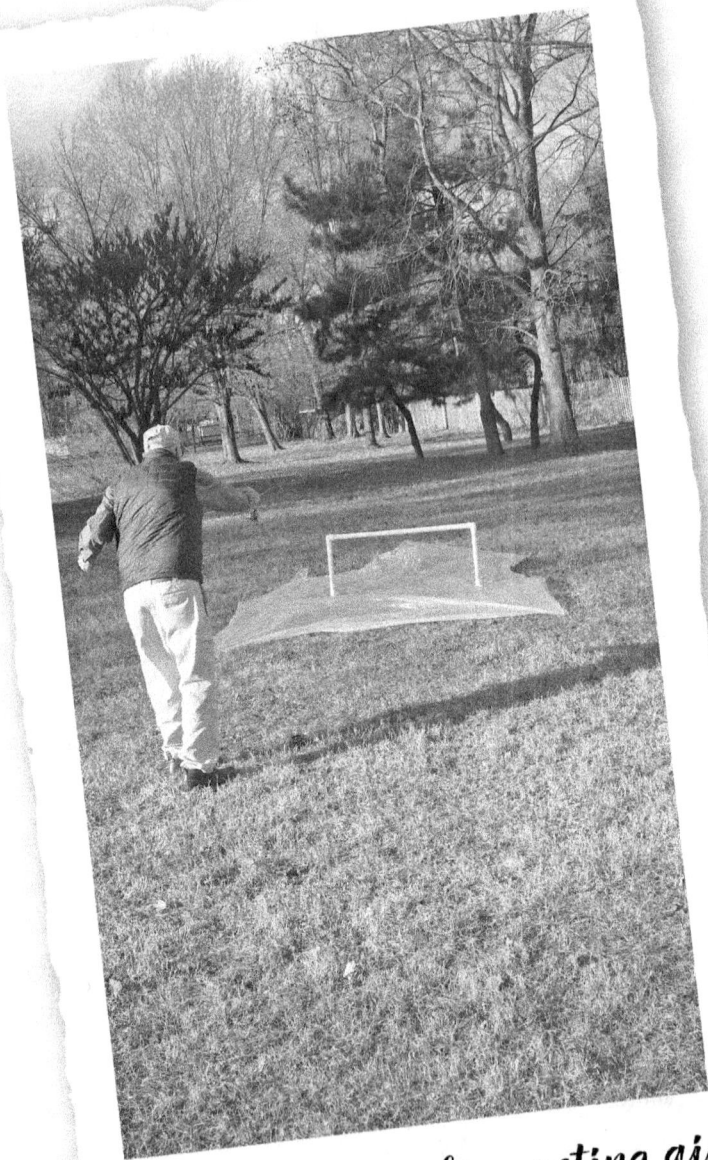

Doyle practices his casting aim.

Improving Your Aim

WHEN YOU CAN'T FISH, PRACTICE CASTING

Looking out my front window on a beautiful year's end morning, I could see that the sun was shining brightly and the wind calm. My eyes settled on my skiff in the driveway, covered with its blue winter-weather blanket. I casually mused that with a little effort I could pull the cover, hook up the trailer and be on the water inside of 20 minutes. Then I casually mentioned the thought to Deborah, my long-suffering wife.

"Great idea," she said. "It's all the way up to 35 degrees, and while you're out there you might help DNR look for the guy that fell overboard near the Bay Bridge the other day. They haven't found him yet."

"I wasn't serious," I countered, "just wishing."

My real situation was that I was still recovering from the abdominal surgery in early December and forbidden by doctor's orders from activities that involved lifting anything heavier than a six-pack for at least three more weeks. Launching a boat was out of the question, and springtime had never seemed so far away.

I reminded myself that next best thing to fishing was playing with fishing tackle, and I had made promises to myself last season to improve a number of skills. One was my casting accuracy. Lawn casting is a low-impact exercise that would get me out of the house and keep me active.

I especially needed to work on placing a bait or lure under piers and docks where perch and rockfish hold during warmer months to beat the heat of the climbing sun.

I had once thought that the fish moved from shallow water structures to deeper water as the sun rose, especially with a falling tide. However, an accomplished skinny-water angler named Woody Tillery dispelled that idea. Woody's strategy was based on his experience that, as the sun rose, the fish felt exposed and so tended to congregate in the cooler shaded areas under the piers and docks. The shade rendered the fish mostly invisible to marauding osprey and herons.

Anglers, however, could cast into those shady refuges as the water level under the structures fell.

Using that strategy, his score of white perch was quite impressive in both numbers and size, despite the often shallow depths, and often included a surprising number of keeper rockfish. It was quite a revelation at the time.

But I found that type of casting was far from an easy task. An angler needs to practice to become adept, and that is not an on-the-water project. Freeing one's bait tangled on a pier gets tiresome after the first three or four iterations. It is an old angling axiom that you can either fish or practice casting, but you can't do both at the same time.

I addressed my accuracy issue by constructing light, easily transportable ersatz dock structure with some modified cardboard boxes and constructed PVC plumbing pipe. Setting up the apparatus on the lawn or a convenient (and vacant) parking lot, I am practicing casting to and under the target. It's a challenging and rewarding task. The wrist snap necessary to keep the lure trajectory low and accurate is not simple. However, I expect to up my score.

Other techniques for working under or close to these types of structure include flipping, skipping, pitching and shooting.

Look them up on any internet bass-fishing site. All can be practiced on that same apparatus and are demonstrated in a number of YouTube videos (search *fishing docks*). I plan on upping my score considerably.

Black Squirrels in the Branches

The snowflakes cascading into my yard are actually a lovely sight, especially since my fireplace is blazing and everyone inside is toasty, including me. There aren't many places I'd rather be right now.

Out this morning on the newly white landscape, I immediately noticed our latest resident. I have finally persuaded my black squirrel buddy onto our front yard treeline. Having been lured with copious amounts of sunflower seeds, beginning last summer, he (squirrel genders are obvious) has finally moved from the backyard area into a more visible location, out front.

Being quick to spot, he makes an interesting visual counterpoint to the rowdy bunch of grays that chase each other up and down the trees in front, occasionally falling out, bouncing on the ground and bounding back up into the upper reaches. The eastern gray squirrel, of which the black squirrel is simply a recessive color variant, mates twice a year, each spring and each fall. I've noticed, however, that they all often mistake springtime for any warm spell that occurs during the long winter months.

One story that explains the numerous presence of this black phase of the eastern gray squirrel posits that a number of black squirrels were released by Teddy Roosevelt in the District of Columbia from a gift of the little critters from admirers in Canada. They subsequently spread out but remain quite populous in the District to this day, maintaining a solid presence in many of the parks of our nation's capital. This resulted in the black phase becoming more numerous than the grays until agricultural practices of the newly arriving colonists thinned out the forested areas and the balance turned back to the grays.

In my community, there's always a black squirrel or two among the grays about every other block, and I'm told that the Eastern Shore has a few areas where large numbers of black squirrels have remained resident in many locations. They are generally regarded as good luck and an interesting addition to the local fauna. If you're interested in seeing them up close, they're quite fond of sunflower seeds.

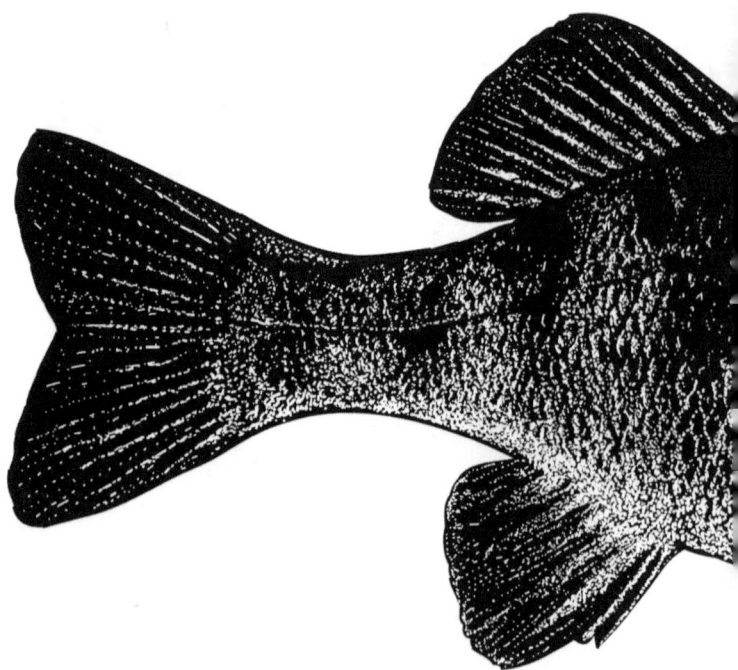

January

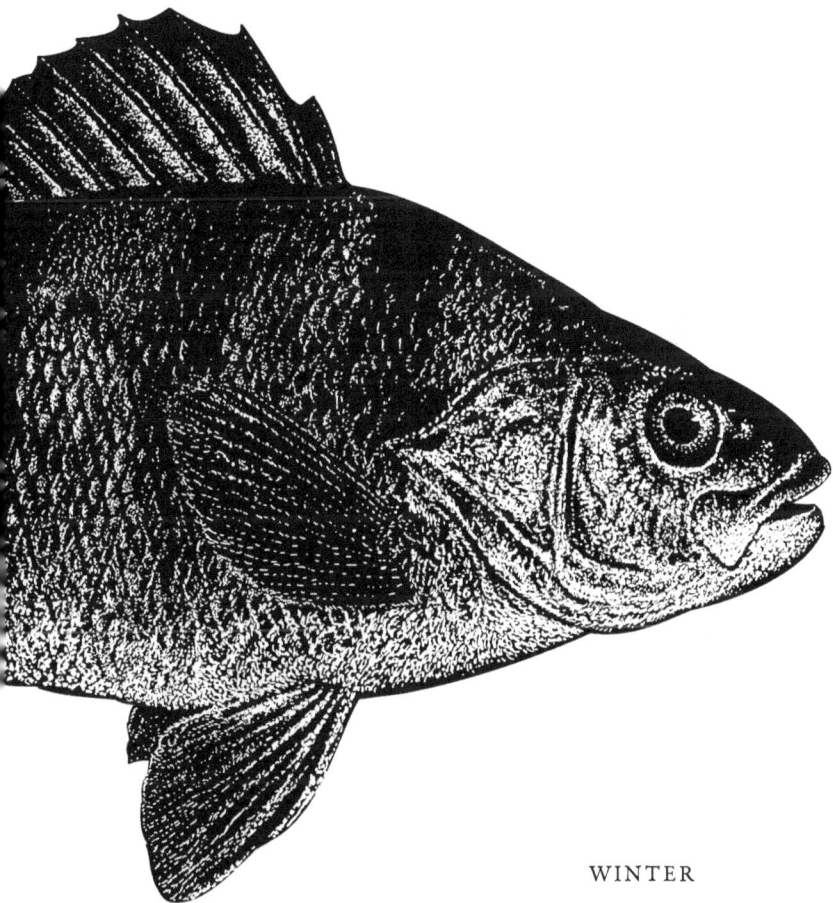

WINTER

The Old Florida fly reel
is a very well-made clone
of the Tibor reels.

How I Keep My New Year's Resolutions

IF MY SUCCESS-RATIO CONTINUES,
THIS WILL BE A VERY GOOD YEAR

New Year's Resolutions are a dicey affair. They generally ignore past behavioral patterns suggesting that those particular promises, intended for self-improvement, won't be kept for very long.

For me such problems are a thing of the past, for I have developed a new approach to my New Year's resolutions. I cannot recommend this strategy to everyone, but I have to say it has certainly improved my quality of life, which is the object of self-improvement efforts, right?

A decade or so ago, after endless cycles of promissory failure, my sole New Year's resolution was that I would henceforth make only personal-improvement commitments that I would be likely to perform, such as resolving to fish or hunt at least two days a week; or seeking out new outdoor experiences and finding a new sporting destination each season.

Lesser goals such as losing 15 pounds, exercising at least three times a week and limiting my intake of adult beverages to weekends or special occasions were transitioned to an indefinite time much later in the calendar year so as not to cloud the focus of the holidays.

Ever since, my success ratio on keeping New Year's Resolutions increased dramatically.

In light of my past successes, this year I have also expanded the scope of my New Year's resolutions to include certain acquisitional goals in my efforts to improve. Working part-time at a sporting goods store, I am probably more aware than most outdoor enthusiasts of the effort and expense that boat, outdoor-clothing and fishing-tackle manufacturers bear to create new and more exciting equipment to enhance our sporting adventures.

It seems in keeping with the spirit of their commitment that I should endeavor to acquire and use more of the superb equipment they have so diligently created. Considering the level of quality and the expense involved in their development and manufacture, the cost of such high-end, high-tech items is reasonable, if not totally justifiable. That's what I tell myself and my wife.

Affording such articles as I now have in mind, among them a fly rod, demand sacrifice on my part. I expect to have to forego a new suit and a pair of dress shoes and to make my neckties last yet another year.

I may also have to cut back on home-improvement projects and forsake having my pickup detailed in order to acquire the new butterfly deep-jigging outfits developed by Shimano. But this sort of self-denial seems appropriate in the scheme of things.

THE BIG PICTURE

Among benefits of my new-found ability to keep to New Year's resolutions, I have also noted a significant increase in my self-esteem.

This is not only reason to celebrate but also to commit to resolutions expanding other horizons in the coming year.

Perhaps something that has to do with tropical destinations during February might be appropriate. The Republic of Panama is especially beckoning.

Going into this new year, I can only hope that I am able to maintain the resolution success level I have achieved in past years. Should you follow my example, I wish you the same high success I have experienced. For I've found that the whole year goes better when I keep my New Year's resolutions.

Happy New Year!

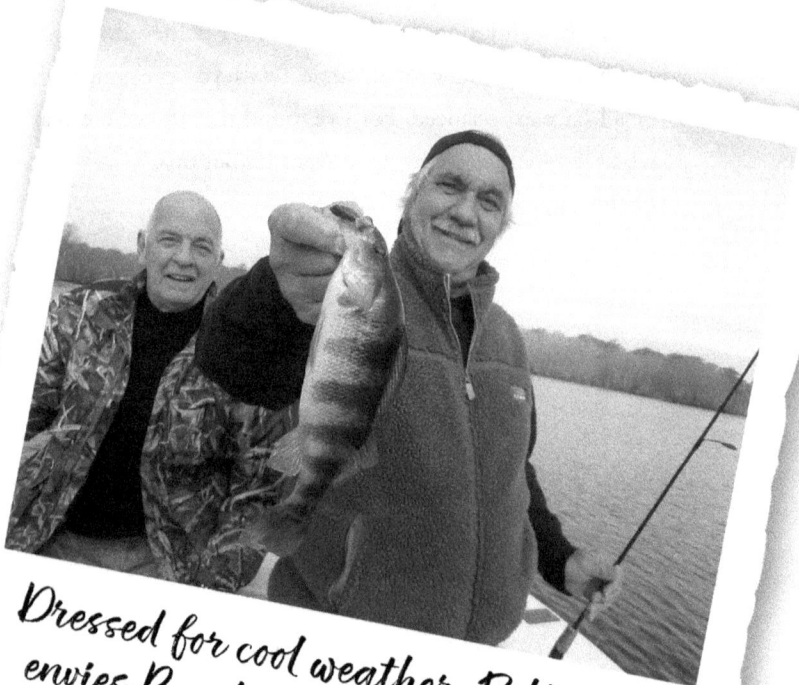

Dressed for cool weather, Bill Doyle envies Randy Steck's yellow perch.

Get the Jump on the Season

ALREADY, YELLOW PERCH—AND WHITE, TOO—ARE
GATHERING IN THE TRIBUTARY HEADWATERS TO SPAWN.

It's starting now. The yellow perch run is on the way, with the white right behind it. Regardless of weather, the season is opening up.

Hardier practitioners will reap the first and richest bounties, as always, so don't be misled by freezing temperatures. The fish may hesitate during periods of extreme cold, but not for long.

Temperature is not the primary element affecting the coming and going of fish. They're also driven by the increasing sunlight, lunar phases, tidal flows and the inexorable changes in their bodies. Females are already swelled to bursting from the copious quantities of roe they are producing. Males are overflowing with milt.

Staging areas are the right places to target, the deeper water up in the tributaries where the schools of fish will build nests waiting whatever secret signal their species need to start for the headwaters to spawn. Yellow perch prefer 45-to-55-degree water for reproducing. Improbable as it seems, on a sunny, 60-degree day, the shallows of a tributary can easily reach those temperatures, though Bay waters may remain in the 30s.

If nothing else, it's time to break out your spring perch-fishing tackle and get it ready for action. Light lines need replacing more frequently than heaver tests, so check yours. If any appear chalky, stiff or in any way suspicious, replace them now. Four-to-six-pound test is the way to go this time of year. Each spool refill at a local sports store costs less than $10.

You'll also need some warm clothes: hip waders or high boots if you're a bank angler, some warm wool gloves (fingerless are best) and a few hand warmers, just in case. If using minnows for bait, don't forget a small bait net. Nothing will numb your hands faster than having to plunge them repeatedly into your live bucket for baits.

A 5-gallon pail remains the most common and best general tackle container, bait bucket, fish holder and sometime-seat for when the bite may be slow. A thermos full of a hot beverage can also go a long way to making the cold more bearable.

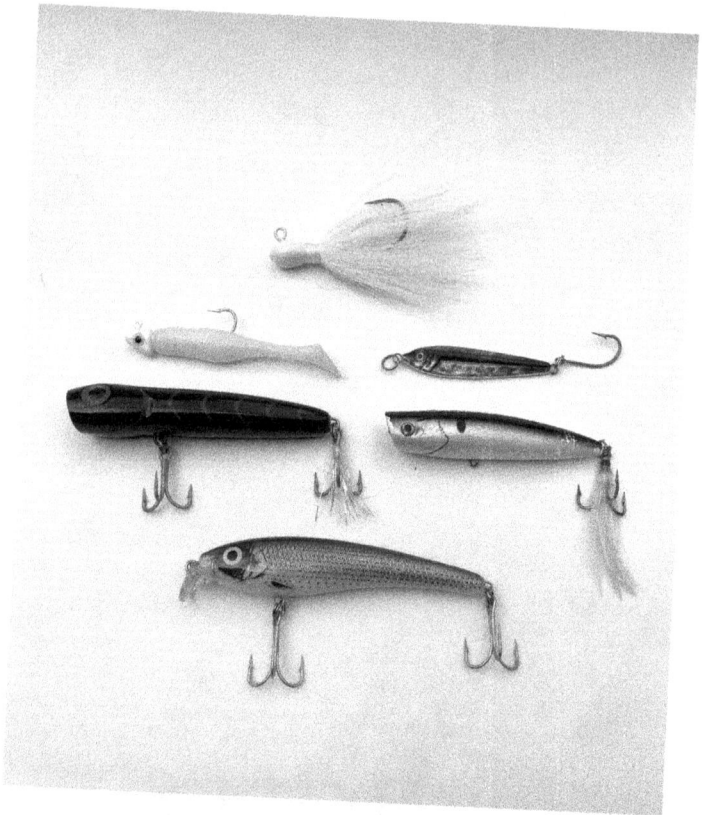

Six dynamic rockfish lures.

Rockfish Dreamin' on a Winter's Day

FIVE MUST-HAVE BAY ROCKFISH LURES

Winter is the time to review your tackle inventory. Once the season starts—and that's just weeks away—there will be many other things to distract you. You won't want to get into a situation on the water that requires a lure that you don't have. So equip yourself with a few of each of these rockfish baits that have consistently produced over many years on the Chesapeake.

FISHING BY THE NUMBERS

The No. 1 all-around rockfish lure has to be the bucktail jig. The classic artificial bait for all occasions, it has undoubtedly, over time, caught more stripers (and probably more fish in general) than any other single lure. It can be cast, trolled, jigged, bounced and drifted.

It can be fished simple or tipped with live bait, strip bait, pork rind or soft plastic attractors. With just this one lure and the correct technique, you can always put fish in the box. Basic colors for the Bay are white, yellow and chartreuse, though the jigs are crafted in every color humans have imagined. A selection of sizes from one-quarter to 2 ounces will cover just about every condition in the Tidewater.

The No. 2 bait on the Bay is the soft plastic jig. It can be fished like the bucktail jig and has become increasingly popular since the first lure of this type (Mann's Stingray Grub) made the jump from freshwater to saltwater a half century ago.

Bass Assassins and BKDs (Bass Kandy Delight) are the overwhelming favorites in the mid-Bay. Zoom Super Flukes, Fin-S, Mister Twisters and the Berkley Gulp! series are surefire fish-foolers as well. The best colors for the Bay, in order of popularity, are lavender over pearl-gray, chartreuse glitter, lavender with silver glitter over pearl-gray, white, chartreuse, yellow and pink.

The No. 3 lure for Chesapeake outings has become the swim bait, a relative newcomer to the lure scene. Tsunami and Storm lure companies make the more popular of these deadly attractors, but plenty more manufacturers are providing competition. Life-like baitfish imitations in varying colors are molded in soft plastic over a strategically weighted hook. These lures are designed to move with a shimmering, swimming motion when retrieved. They have proven irresistible to stripers throughout the Bay.

The No. 4 artificial fish-fooler is the Stingsilver-type vertical job. The 2-ounce size is the most widely used, but the lure is available and effective in sizes from one-quarter to over 4 ounces from a variety of manufacturers. The best colors seem to be silver, gold, chartreuse green over yellow, chartreuse and white.

This lure is often augmented with a smaller teaser jig or a fly tied 12- to 18-inches up to the leader. Jigged just off the bottom, this lure is probably the top producer of light-tackle fish caught in deep water from late summer well into fall.

The No. 5 rockfish lure, and the most exciting to use, is the top-water plug. Rockfish react to the lure with visibly explosive strikes, often with numerous near-misses making this bait the most nerve-challenging and visually spectacular of all the artificial baits on the Chesapeake.

The Stillwater Smack-it and Smack-It Jr. have become the most popular of these surface-action lures. Distant seconds, but still very effective, are the Storm Saltwater Chug Bug, the Heddon Spook series and, more recently, the Chug Norris.

Manufactured with floating plastic bodies, they are baitfish-shaped, 5- to 6-inches, with a concave mouth designed to make a popping sound, throw water, sputter and otherwise create a noisy surface disturbance that draws rockfish attention from considerable distances.

These top-water plugs are particularly effective in early spring on the shallow flats of the Susquehanna, any time fish are feeding on the surface and in the fall around the mouths of the tributaries in the mornings and evenings. The best colors have been blue over pearl, olive over gold, black over pearl, chartreuse green over fluorescent yellow and all black.

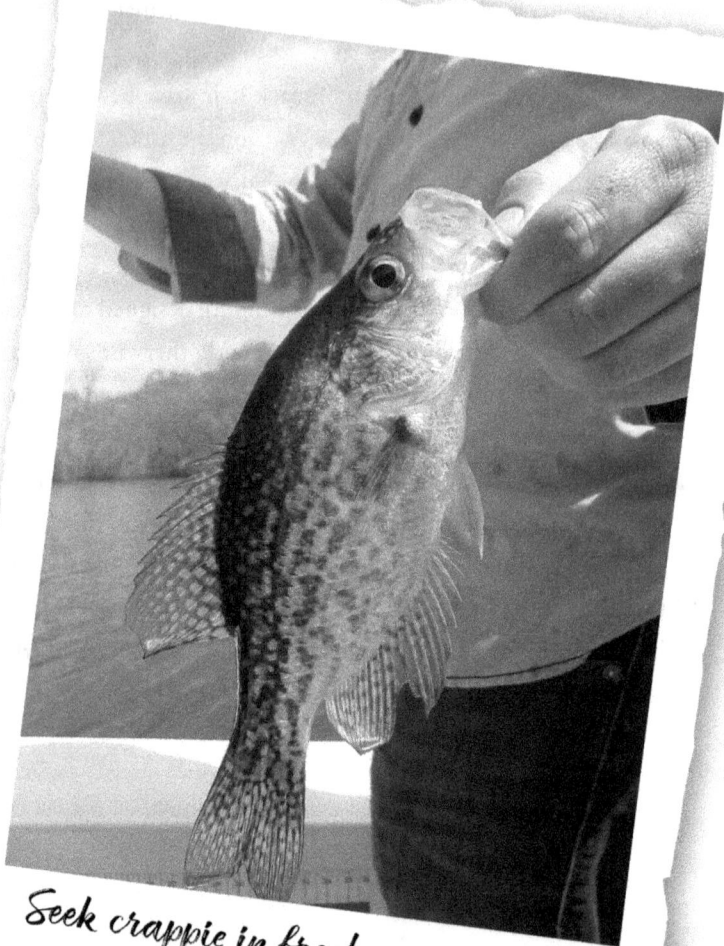

Seek crappie in fresher tributaries as well as fresh water.

Eager for the Coming Season

THE FIRST FISH OF THE YEAR START MOVING IN FEBRUARY

Yes, I know temperatures have plunged into single digits lately, but it's best to consider these events as just the last freeze before the thaw. The days are getting longer with more and more sunlight and already a number of finned species are beginning to respond. February is only a week away, and that's when yellow perch begin staging to ascend the tributaries to spawn. That's a cause to rejoice.

It's not too soon to get out a light spin rod, freshen your reel spools with 4- or 6-pound monofilament, dig out some top/bottom rigs, arm them with No. 4 hooks and a few light sinkers and ready yourself for the new season. The yellow perch now schooling will be fat and frisky.

A kayak, canoe or any small light craft is excellent for searching out groups of the yellow neds. If you're skeptical about using a kayak in colder weather, recall that Eskimos developed the craft for use in the Arctic. Dress warmly and explore just outside the mouths of the upper tributaries for the deeper holes, 15 to 30 feet. An electronic fish finder will be very handy in locating the fish. But slowly drifting and bouncing a lip-hooked minnow or a grass shrimp on a small jig can also zero in on a honey hole.

Later in February, when the perch ascend the smaller creeks and streams, they can be reached from the shore. At this time you'll want to add some bobbers and bright-colored shad darts to your tackle to target the shallower waters with the same baits.

Yellows like temperatures in the 40s to begin their spawn. But a day of full sun can boost the shallows up 10 degrees in no time, so don't wait for especially sultry days. The northern edges of the tributaries, getting the most sun, warm earliest.

Males invariably arrive at the spawning sites first. The females will tarry a week or so, spawning two to three times before returning downstream. The males will leave only after the females stop showing up. The run will continue well into April.

Minimum size for yellow perch is 9 inches with a possession limit of ten fish. A 14-incher is a citation.

As the yellow perch spawn starts to slow, the white perch begin to arrive. All of the same tackle and techniques do the job nicely. There is no minimum size nor possession limit.

Later in February and into March, the crappie become active and begin gathering in schools. Crappie, which are highly regarded on the table, are most often found in fresh water. But the fresher areas of the tributaries will yield fish as well. The key to finding concentrations of these fish—also called calico bass, specs, slabs and sac-a-lait—is simple: Target anywhere there are brush or tree overhangs, laydowns or submerged growths of vegetation.

Larger fish become more active in early morning and in the evenings. They can also be targeted with artificial lights at night. Small minnows under a bobber are perfect. Crappie have large mouths with a delicate construction, which gives them yet another alias, papermouths. Maintain a deft touch when fighting these scrappers.

Pickerel are last on the early springtime list. A long, slender and toothy fish, the grass pike is a splendid fighter and is energized by colder weather. Taking spoons, spinner baits and crank baits with abandon, these fish are also total suckers for a lip-hooked minnow slowly trolled under a small bobber. Pickerel flesh is firm and white, but is so bony that most anglers return them to the water.

Monofilament in the 10-pound range is more than enough to bring these fish to hand, though a net is recommended in light of their teeth.

Pickerel are an ambush predator, so docks, piers, laydowns or any kind of submerged structure will attract and hold them. Later in March, find them schooling and preparing their own spawn.

Minimum size is 14 inches with a five-fish limit in fresh water and a ten-fish limit in the Bay and tributaries. A 36-incher is a citation.

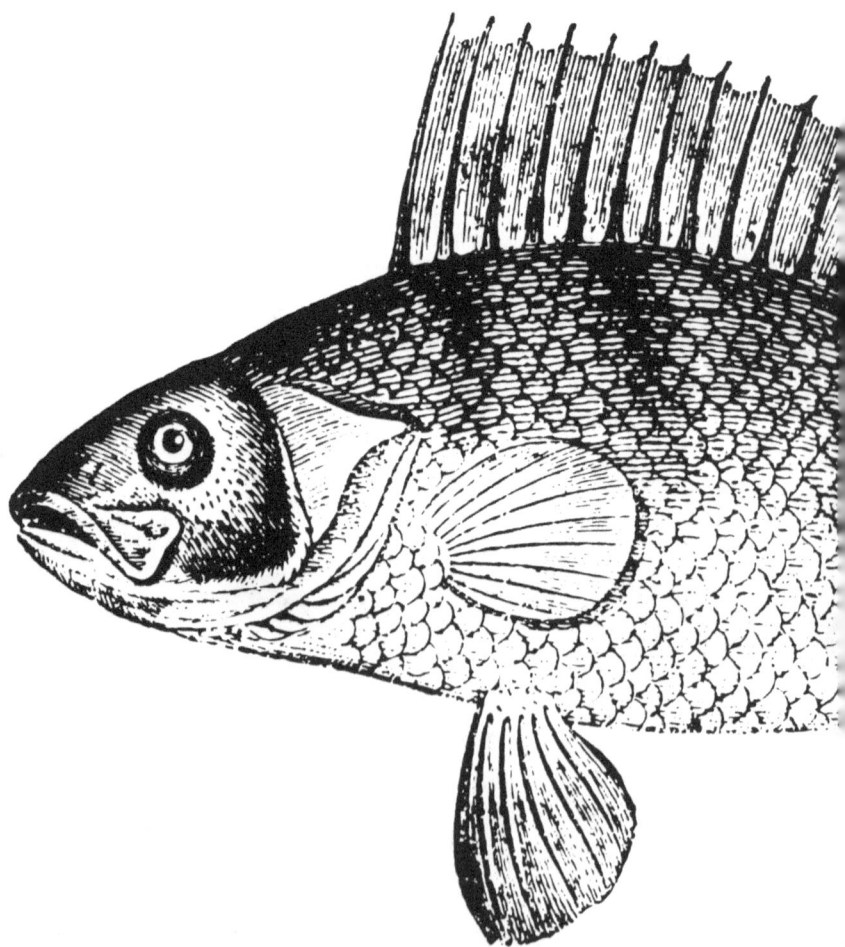

February

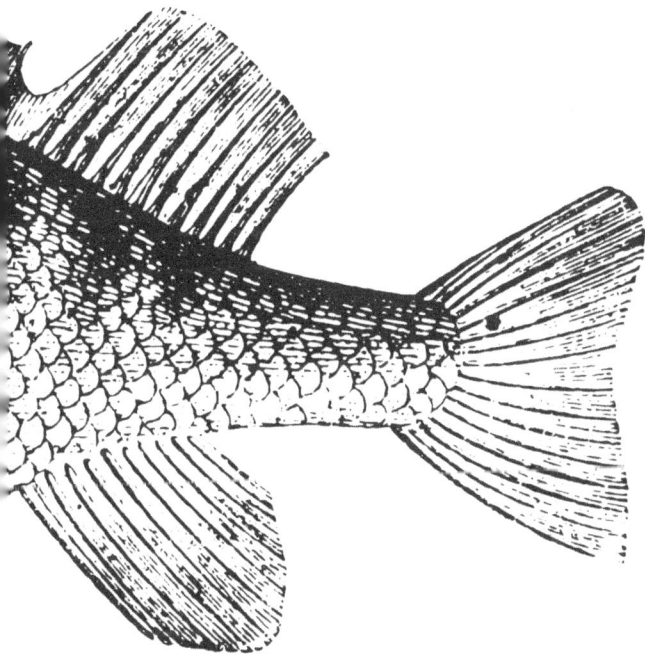

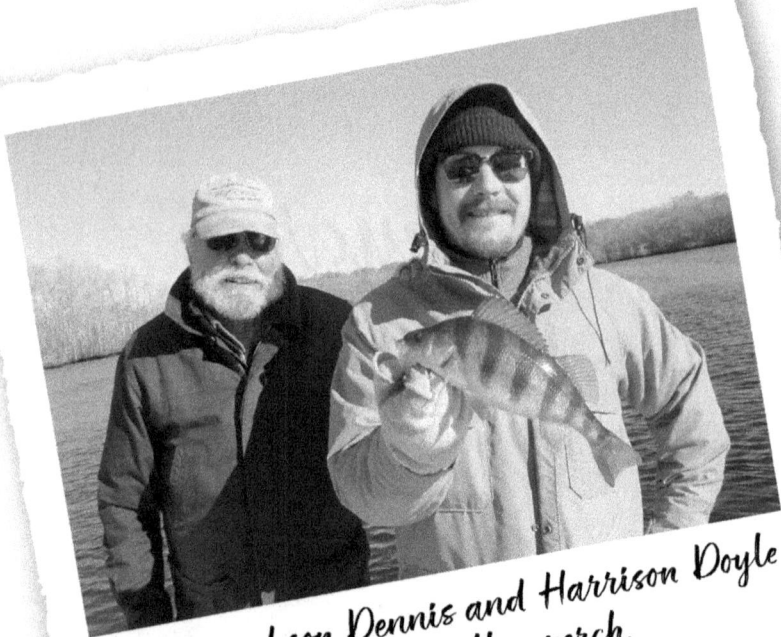

Father and son Dennis and Harrison Doyle gloat over a yellow perch.

Start the New Year with the Yella Fellas

THIS ANGLER'S SPRING ARRIVES EARLY

Flipping my small, gold spoon out from the stream bank, I said a prayer to the fish gods. The winter had been hard on my disposition; my wife had just recommended, she had demanded actually, that I get out of the house and onto the water. So here I was.

The tide was dropping a bit, just right for this stretch of the Tuckahoe, a particularly fertile Eastern Shore tributary of the mighty Choptank. The bottom was barely discernible near the shoreline and out of sight anywhere deeper than 18 inches. I liked that. Murky water relaxes the fish, as it masks them from airborne predators.

I scanned the far bank. The stark, black, leafless trees edging the water did not lend much comfort to a chilly landscape, but the chocolate-shaded water, moving slowly in front of me, was rich with possibilities.

I warned myself not to expect anything on this first outing in early February. After all, fishing for early yellow perch is a crap shoot. Some days you get 'em, but usually you don't, and you'll never know which it will be until you're ready to go home. With that semi-profound thought, my rod tip twitched.

Was it a fish, or had I just bumped bottom? I lowered the rod and let my spoon settle back. It was sweetened with a small, lip-hooked mummichog, a yellow ned's favorite treat.

I hoped that the wobbling of the descending combined with the fresh, wriggling minnow I would prove irresistible to any cruising perch. But this time it didn't. Finally I lifted my rod, felt no resistance and once again slowly retrieved the lure, weaving it lazily back through the light current.

FIRST FISH

Apparently the departing meal was more than the unseen perch could endure. It finally and recklessly gobbled the minnow and my spoon and headed out for the opposite shore. My light rod bent almost in half as my spirits soared and the reel groaned.

My chill-stung fingers were suddenly warm, and my chest was pounding. This angler's spring had just arrived on the Tidewater. Nervously playing the fish like it was a world record in progress, I eased it gingerly toward my position on the bank.

As the fish neared, gold flashes telegraphed from the cloudy water, confirming the species. My first yellow perch of the year was at hand. It would not do to lose it now; that could queer the whole season, though I will always deny being superstitious about such things.

Ever so gently, I lifted the fish nearer and nearer, finally sliding it up onto the bank. It flopped angrily, displaying its bright spawning colors and emphasizing that it had no intention of cooperating with anything I had in mind.

I reached down, carefully avoiding its erect spiny dorsal fin, and unhooked the frisky devil. It was a bright male, just under the legal size of 9 inches and with a supply of milt that was obviously overflowing. I admired it a bit and then slid it back into the Tuckahoe to go about its business. All was now right with the world. I had scored my first yella fella.

MEET PERCA FLAVESCENS

The yellow perch is the first fish of the year to make its spawning run in the Tidewater. Its scientific name, perca flavescens, translates as dusky, turning to gold, though for years I thought it meant flavorful perch. I still think my original guess was the more apt. A particularly handsome creature, it is dark green on top with seven dark vertical bars along gold-colored flanks. It sports bright orange swim fins, especially during the spawn when it ventures up into the freshest parts of Bay tributaries.

In the better areas, principally the headwaters and feeder streams of the Bush, Chester, Wye and Choptank on the Eastern Shore and the Gunpowder and Patuxent on the western side, good populations can be encountered in the early spring.

Target the deeper waters up in the tributaries where yellow perch schools will build their nests awaiting whatever secret signal their instincts await to start the spawn. Neds (a yellow perch nickname) prefer 45- to 55-degree water for reproducing. Improbably as it seems, on a sunny, 60-degree day in January or February, the shallows of a tributary can reach those temperatures, though Bay waters may remain in the 30s.

THE BEST TOOLS FOR THE JOB

A 7-foot medium-weight spin rod is adequate for pan fishing like this. However, maybe this spring is time to invent in a 6-to-6.5-foot light- or ultra-light-action rod matched with one of the many 1000-series spin reels. It is far more satisfying to use tackle matched to the fish, and casting the lightweight lures and baits you'll be using will be far easier. Your accuracy will be vastly improved, and light bites will be far more detectable.

The best terminal setup is a pair of shad darts about 18 inches below a small weighted casting bobber. You can tip the darts with grass shrimp, minnows, bookworms, earthworms, butter worms or any combination. The possession limit is ten fish of at least 9 inches in length per day.

The yella fellas won't disappoint you on your line or on the table.

DREDGE, FRY AND ENJOY

They, like white perch, are best prepared cleaned, rolled in panko crumbs and fried in hot peanut or corn oil until golden brown. Many devotees insist that yellow perch are better than white, though that argument could be endless.

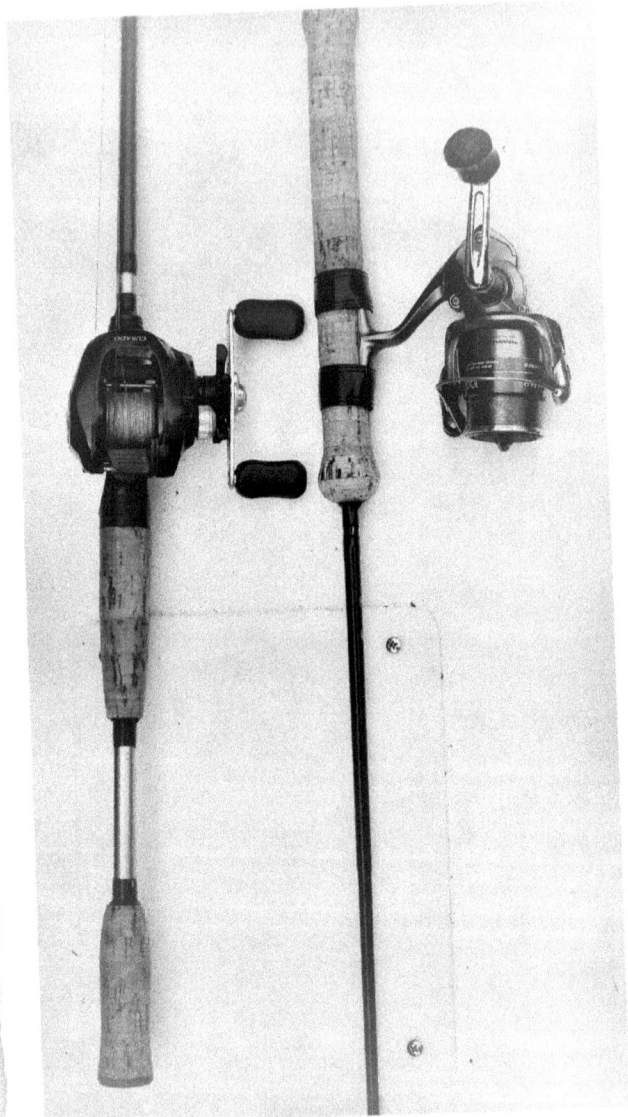

Two customized rod handles.

Customize Your Rod, Part 1

HOW TO MAKE THE ROD YOU NEED

There are essentially two types of light-tackle sport-fishing reels, spinning and casting. The spin reel has a fixed-line spool mechanism mounted below the rod. Line is evenly wound onto the reel spool by an armature that circles the spool. Lures and baits are cast out by disengaging the armature, allowing the line to be pulled off the cylindrical spool with little or no resistance as the lure is thrown. Virtually tangle free and easy to use, the spin reel is the most popular type in use.

The casting reel, in contrast, is more compact than the spin reel. Positioned above the rod, it utilizes a revolving spool mechanism that retrieves and holds the line. Lures and baits are cast out by putting the reel into free spool, then throwing the lure. The lure's weight pulls the line out of the turning spool. The spool's revolutions are controlled by built-in feathering mechanisms plus some delicate angler thumb pressure that prevents line tangles.

Working a rocky shoreline last fall for white perch with a light finesse-actioned casting outfit, I was once again disappointed. The newly acquired rig didn't cast the light one-sixth-ounce spinner bait very far or with any amount of accuracy. Yet this rod was clearly marked for lures as light as one-eighth ounce, and the reel was optimally tuned for light lures. I had been experiencing this problem for some time with a number of different casting rigs.

Why didn't I turn to ultra-light spin tackle, as the primary advantage of a spinning outfit is no resistance to throwing virtually any weight lure? Birds-nests (aka backlashes or spool overruns), the bane of all casting-gear fans, are rare.

I would have made that choice if all anglers were of a uniformly logical and mentally balanced nature. Unfortunately that is not nearly the situation, especially among ultra-light tackle fanatics. A few of us are nuts, at least when it comes to tackle preferences.

I wanted the extra control a casting reel gives in adjusting for range and direction with properly applied thumb pressure. I admire the exacting nature of the reel, with its complex, delicate gears and spool-braking mechanisms. Its fish-fighting drag system is far smoother, stronger and more sensitive, and I'm fond of the fine whirring noise the reel makes as the line speeds out on a long cast. Also, the learned skill that it takes to continually work a shoreline, cast after cast without incident, is rewarding in itself.

After musing on the problem, I decided on an experiment. Putting a small, low-profile casting reel onto a 6-foot ultra-light action spin rod marked for a minimum lure size of one-sixteenth ounce, I tied a one-sixth ounce lure on my makeshift rig and walked out on my front porch. With a casual effort, I sent the bait flying the length of my yard, completely over the front street and well into the bushes of the house across from me. Those spin rod specifications were the solution to my quest.

Researching the catalogs of every rod manufacturer I could think of, I discovered another interesting situation. No casting rods manufactured could mimic that rod action or that lure range. None; not even close.

Continuing to use the casting reel on the spin rod was not a realistic solution because the guides did not align properly with the reel and the reel seat was in an awkward location. But that was a minor problem because I know that it's simple to make a fishing rod of just about any specification yourself.

Accessing a rod-building website and choosing a couple of spin-rod blanks of the type I desired, plus the cork handles and reel seats that were appropriate for a casting reel, some rod epoxy and the proper thread and correct rod guides, I called in an order, sat back and waited for my items to arrive.

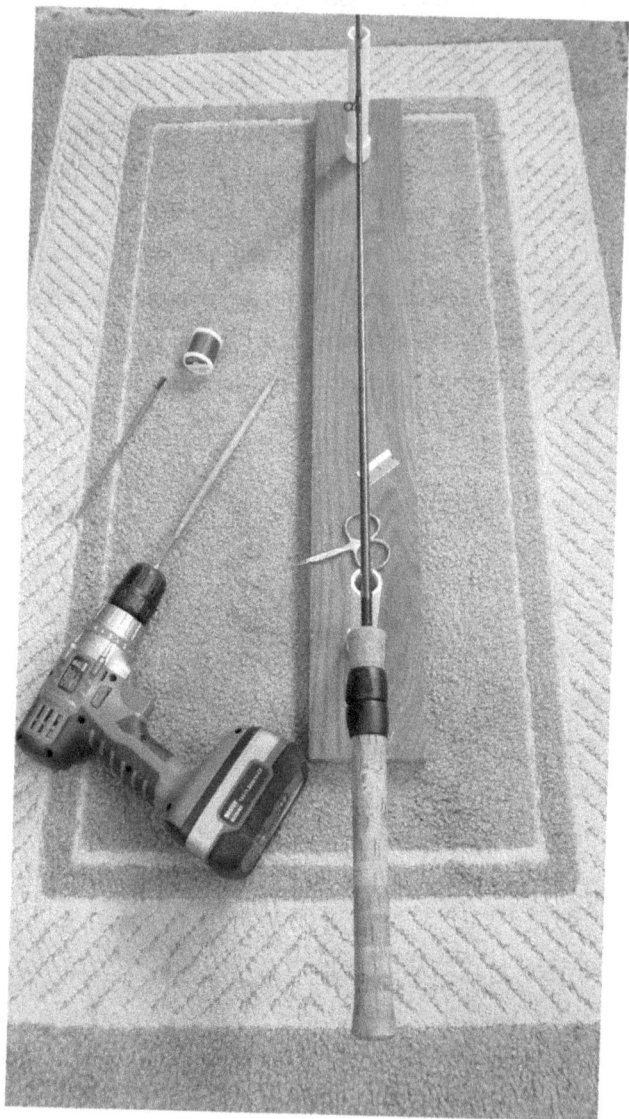

Rod and rod holder with drill,
file and other hand tools.

Customize Your Rod, Part 2

RODS MADE TO TASTE REMAIN WORKS IN PROGRESS

The wind was still howling through the trees when my rod-building components arrived. I pulled my coat tighter against my chest as I exited my home for the mailbox.

Back inside, I spewed the contents across the dining room table, thankful that my wife had already left for the day. There was an ultra-light-action rod blank, 6 feet long and rated for 2-to-4-pound line and one-thirty-second to one-fourth ounce baits. Also included were the proper set of eight casting rod guides, rod-wrapping thread, finishing epoxy, a couple of disposable brushes and a simple cork reel-seat handle.

The rod handle had been pre-assembled out of cork rings and tapered just as I desired. But the hole bored in the handle was considerably smaller than the blank I received. So I ventured out into my wife's sculpturing studio to look for some appropriately sized rat-tail files.

I came upon them almost immediately, held in a bucket of other implements she had used in a recent sculpting project. Two of the files were exactly the size I was looking for: clear proof to me of the gods' good wishes, as her studio is maintained as only another artist can appreciate in that organization is anathema to creativity.

Fixing the base of the file in a portable drill, I walked into the kitchen and, holding the handle over the waste bucket, bored out the internal channel to just the right size for the tapered rod butt. Slathering the butt end of the blank with some 15-minute epoxy, I gave it a little time to be sure it was getting a good grip on the blank, then slid the cork handle down over the blank and into place.

Placing the blank and handle onto a cradle that I had earlier constructed out of scrap lumber and PVC tubing parts, I began to wind on the casting-rod guides. I closely monitoring the wrap on each guide foot, making sure I kept each thread turn firmly touching the previous to achieve a neat and appealing wrap. I remembered that task as taking an hour or so; this time, it took over four hours.

Applying the guide-wrap finish was a simple task. Slowly mixing to avoid air bubbles in the two-part epoxy, I carefully applied a layer of finish to each of the guide wraps. As I worked, the rod remained in the wrapping cradle. Once every five minutes for the first half hour, then once every 15 minutes until the epoxy had firmly set with a level finish, I rotated the rod 180 degrees.

I then had a new custom fishing rod, done inexpensively in the comfort of my home and well before my lovely wife returned.

A couple of days later, I put the rod to the test. On the water, I immediately noticed two faults. First, the handle was too short for my style of casting and fish fighting. Secondly, a couple of the guides were not in perfect alignment.

So I am not finished. I tell myself it will be a fairly simple matter to extend the handle with some additional corks over a blank extension and to remove the offending guides and rewrap them.

Rods made to your personal tastes are a work in progress and are done only when you're completely satisfied.

Braided 10-pound test line

20-pound test monofilament line.

The Critical Link Between You and the Fish

THE MOST IMPORTANT ITEM IN YOUR TACKLE INVENTORY IS ALSO THE LEAST EXPENSIVE

A rockfish had just consumed my small, live spot, I knew that it was a good-sized fella from its forceful and deliberate pace.

Having hooked it at the base of a bridge support, I was also prepared for the fish's next move. As it bored away and cornered on the first nearby concrete support, it went right where I expected.

Previously, live-lining spot around the various structures on the Chesapeake, I had lost a heartbreaking number of large rockfish. Almost all were due to encounters with the concrete, rock and steel constructions that had attracted and held the fish in the first place. So I made some changes to my tackle.

Using braided line of approximately 50-pound test, which is about the same diameter as the 20-pound mono, I was not worried by the stress placed on my gear when that hefty rockfish began threading its way through the concrete and rebar jungle gym where I'd hooked it. With my drag set at a moderate level, I gave up a lot of line as I backed my skiff off for a better angle. Then I torqued the drag down firmly, and the game was on.

I could feel the 50-pound braid grating against the intervening bridge supports, but I felt certain the additional coatings and the heavier Power Pro line would hold up. As I levered the fish first around one obstacle then another, my line steadily built back up on the spool and the fish came ever closer. At last the 32-incher came to the net.

This is one case where braid was clearly superior to mono. But as every angler knows, there is no single solution for everything.

Fishing line is the most important item in your tackle inventory. Today the types of line selections are many. Those designed for spinning, casting and trolling tackle range from monofilament, which is translucent, to various braided lines, which are opaque and are sometimes referred to as super lines because of their ultra-high line strength and tiny diameter. Both line options are available in multiple colors, such as clear, tinted, natural, high visibility and fluorescent.

MONOFILAMENT

Monofilament is still the best option for most light-tackle fishing. It's inexpensive and has low visibility. When you're using monofilament, if there's a question as to whether to replace the mono on your reel, yes, replace it. Freshly manufactured monofilament can last only two to three years when well used, even if it is protected from UV rays. But even with the best of care, it won't always retain 100 percent of its qualities. Salt sucks the softening agents out, making it less manageable, and friction from the guides or dragging the line across underwater structure creates weak spots. Wear stress also makes the line more visible to fish.

Mono stretches before it breaks. However, the elasticity of mono can sometimes be an advantage. When rigging my light perch rods for casting spinner baits in the shallows, I always use monofilament. The stretch cushions their fragile mouth structure during the fight, and other perch in the school are far more tolerant to continued casting with the 4-to-6-pound translucent lines.

As to color choices, clear or lightly tinted are superior. If the water is murky, choose a green, gray or blue-tinted line. They are the likeliest to be unnoticed. If water is very clear always go with a clear line.

You want your reel to hold at least 100 yards in freshwater fishing. If you're angling the Bay, 150 yards or more is appropriate.

WHY RISK THE LOSS OF A GOOD FISH
FOR SUCH A MINOR INVESTMENT?

The average spin or casting reel can be respooled with fresh, quality monofilament relatively inexpensively. Monofilament is also not an item to bargain hunt. You want freshly manufactured and on the premium side. Seeking to save money here will at best save you a couple of pennies a yard and at worst cost you a lot of tackle and perhaps the best fish of the season.

Unless you are skilled in spooling lines, have them done at a reputable sports store. Winding line by hand from a bulk spool onto a spinning reel invariably puts a twist in the line. A tackle shop will have a winding machine that puts line directly onto the reel spool without the twist. The shop will also put the correct amount of line on your spool for best casting efficiency and will wind it with uniform tension, another aspect of line spooling that ensures trouble-free use.

BRAIDED LINE

Braided lines, which are made from four to as many as eight strands of woven polyethylene, are much more resilient than mono and retain close to their full properties for a number of years. While more expensive than mono, they do not stretch or wear from UV rays and can definitely result in more fish in the box.

But they are not totally immune to wear. Strip off and discard the first 20 feet of all fishing line from each reel at the start of every year. Examine the spool closely. If you see any line fraying farther down its length, consider replacing it. Braided line bleaches out easily and if you've noticed loss of line color in a section, cut it out or replace it. If any one of its strands has suffered abrasion in any particular place, your overall line test can be affected by as much as 25 to 50 percent.

Trolling mandates a different set of qualities for fishing line. Because of its virtual lack of stretch, braid has superior hook-setting qualities, and its comparatively smaller diameter means less water resistance and increased line capacities on your reels. That translates into getting deeper with less weight and solid hookups trolling very long lines. Bright or fluorescent colors here will make an angler's life easier as the lines streaming aft are easily seen and can be kept from cross and tangling.

Except for the trolling applications, where it is essential to ensure that multiples lines are not crossed or tangled, avoid bright and fluorescent colors. Fish can see them even better than you can. Big fish, particularly, will avoid them.

If you're intent on landing the next big fish you hook, replace your line often and begin new outings by replacing your leaders (fresh line is less visible than used) plus retying your knots, for they eventually wear out. Your break-offs will plummet. I guarantee it.

Four variations of circle hooks, and circle hook close up.

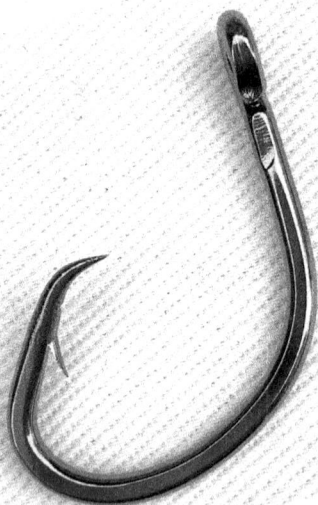

Circle Hooks Save Lives

LEARN TO USE THEM

My experience with circle hooks began decades ago, when I took part in the first Maryland Department of Natural Resources project studying mortality in rockfish caught with J-hooks versus circle hooks. All the fishers were chumming. In the control group, using J-hooks, we established that half of the deep-hooked fish that were released died within two hours. Unfortunately, we deep hooked a significant portion of our catch.

The reason is the design of the J-hook. When the J-hook is swallowed and the fish hooked up, the point often penetrates a nearby vital organ, and that is a sure death sentence. The study concluded that on the whole, circle hooks drastically lessened deep-hooking and had a significantly higher fish survival rate when released. Based on this and similar studies over the years, DNR now mandates circle hooks always be used in chumming and live-lining, the two angling techniques that most often result in deep-hooking fish with the J-hook features.

Yet on first glance the circle hook seems ill designed to be effective at catching fish. The hook point is directed inward, toward the shank of the hook, and would seem to avoid penetration of the fish's mouth. In a subsequent trip to the Smithsonian Institution in Washington, however, I happened on an ancient example of one of the first fishhooks ever used by the Inuit Indians of the Arctic, whose diets consisted mostly of fish. For hundreds of years, it strongly resembled the modern circle hook. What a surprise.

AN OLD FISHERMAN LEARNS NEW TRICKS

This good news for rockfish may require you to learn some new tactics. The most important change in angling technique is allowing only the fish's movements to set the circle hook. Any sudden striking movement, or increased rod pressure by the angler to assist in the hook up, generally resulted in missing it completely.

Dead-sticking your rod, or leaving it in a rod holder until you are sure the fish is hooked, is one sure method. If you insist on holding the rod, you must wait until the fish brings the line tight, then, pointing the rod directly at the fish, crank your reel deliberately until you feel the full weight of the fish on your line and only then deliberately raise your rod to ensure hookup and begin to bring it to hand.

The later summer season proves even more problematic. When dealing with the smaller fish available, I began to miss a distressing number of takes. More fish suffered deep hooking, too, though the majority of those were keepers destined for my fish box. In only one undersized fish, the circle hook stuck in the stomach lining. I eventually managed to work the hook free, but neither the fish nor I was happy.

Rethinking my set-ups, I suspected my choice in hook size may have been faulty. Though the 8/0 circle hooks that I had been using worked flawlessly with larger fish, some of the little guys (with correspondingly smaller mouths and stomachs) ended up with the hooks never entering their mouths or being trapped down in their belly. I increased my inventory of smaller circle hooks all the way down to 3/0. That solved the issue as well as using a hook sized similar to the size of the bait. Leaving the hook point exposed and never burying it deep in the bait will also result in improving positive results.

Knot choices were also among my other problems. I habitually used a loop knot design for normal bait fishing, giving the baits as much free action as possible. This proved a liability with circle hooks, particularly with fish under 24 inches. The smaller hooks and baits needed the addition of a stiff snell knot to assist in directing the baited hook into the corner of the fish's mouth. (A web search for *snell knots* will give you any number of easy-to-tie solutions.)

When live-lining, I've also found that using the snell knot and hooking the bait fish behind rather than in front of the dorsal fin can result in superior hook-ups and more caught fish.

Yes, learning to use circle hooks is a process. You need to experiment and compare your results. Your rewards are becoming a better fisherman—and having more fish to keep you at it year after year.

Doyle celebrates one reward of a fishing life.

Benefits of a Fishing Life

THE GODS DO NOT SUBTRACT FROM AN ALLOTTED LIFESPAN THE HOURS SPENT FISHING

There is hardly any human activity more restorative, calming, comforting and just plain relaxing than a day on the water attempting to convince a fish to bite your line.

Fishing promises quiet contemplation, fine scenery and communion with nature with the outside chance of scoring a healthy meal.

It is not a particularly strenuous sport. Other than casting out your bait or lure, most of your time and attention is spent waiting for the fish to decide whether or not to eat it. That pretty much puts any pressure for success directly in the hands or fins of the fish, leaving your mind free to wander.

Search the word *fishing* online, and you'll get over a half-billion hits. The next most popular sport, golfing, scores scarcely five percent of that number. Not bad for a game that simply requires at its most basic, a pole, some string, a hook and a worm and a good-looking piece of water.

Children take to fishing like few other activities, which is proof positive of its basically pure and simple nature. Older men revel in its intricacies and total absorption of the self.

I have devoted a great portion of my life to chasing fish and have never regretted a single moment. In fact, I'm a firm believer in the adage, *You* can never fish too much; it just can't be done.

That may be the reason that the sport is so consuming and restive. It gives opportunity for philosophical reflection without the actual decision to indulge in such highbrow activity.

I'm having trouble staying asleep through the night. That happens this time of year. Probably because of the pollen starting to pour off the surrounding trees, my sinuses are seizing up and threatening to suffocate me in the wee hours. But I know it's not so simple.

The growing warmth and lengthening days make a subconscious call to action. Spring is here and trophy rockfish season will soon arrive.

What is it about fishing that so fulfills me? It doesn't take me long to answer. A sporting life is nothing if not rich in memories.

Long ago, with the first blush of a rising sun off a rocky point in the Chesapeake, a gentle wind with a mighty feeding boil from a big striper out in front resulted in a surge of adrenaline that burned the scene into a memory lasting over 50 years.

The trophy rockfish season is an opportunity for major memories. As I insist on light tackle, my success rate this time of year is hardly noteworthy. But some years I do get it done, and the experience is worth every bit of my time and effort. The click of a reel as the spool turns, slowly at first, then ever quicker, has an effect on my pulse like nothing else.

I feel a special intensity when the line finally comes tight with the first surge of a rockfish that may just be more powerful than me. And the quickening creep of panic as I desperately try to keep things under control, especially when it's impossible. That's the stuff that keeps me coming back year after year.

The little guys create big moments, too. A bull bluegill no more than 11 inches can make my breath stop when it smashes a small popping bug, turns its big flat side to me, then strips all of my loose fly line in a mad flurry ending with a run that sets the drag on my small fly reel chattering like an angry bluejay. That is a definite moment. The first run of a thick white perch that's smashed your small spinnerbait or wet fly on ultra-light tackle in Bay shallows is always alarming, especially if you suspect it isn't going to stop.

I've often been advised to tighten up my drag, use heavier line or otherwise jerk 'em in the boat. But I disregard such comments. If you're not losing a few fish, you're doing it wrong. It's not a sport if you always win.

My memories of a special fish lost at the side of the boat after a great struggle always last longer than memories of any I've conquered. I invariably wish those fish well and hope they go on to disappoint others. Knowing their wildness is the gift of which I'll never tire.

Though I have been an outdoor addict virtually since birth and have fished, explored, hunted, paddled, cruised, crept, trudged and crawled through many areas of Maryland's beautiful Tidewater, in hindsight I really had no idea just how bountiful, vast and varied our wonderful state really is. In a recent analysis of self, I'm guessing that in my last 50 years, I've visited just under 20 percent of the better spots in our incredible state.

I've never slept better than after a day on the water; that alone is an important thing in this fast-paced civilization that we've created. Now more than ever, our health and well-being depend on finding ways to relax and take in life.

The principal secret of a happy and contented life: The best time to go fishing is whenever you can.

ACKNOWLEDGMENTS

The first acknowledgement for sources and inspirations for this book and my subsequently extensive sporting life goes to my father, Jack Doyle, and my first fish caught with him, a rather large bluegill as I remember. I can still very clearly recall that event some 75 years ago. The next is to my grandfather, Emory Seib, who taught me how to shoot safely and hunt with guns of all types, starting at age 6, not an insignificant task.

Then, much later comes my wife Deb who stoically endured my endless late-night, long-day and very early-morning passions for chasing tides on the Chesapeake and my endless tales of stripers that I caught and released but rarely brought home. My clothes, stinking of fish, plus a vast collection of arcane fishing gear were the only things that convinced her I was not up to mischief but simply a bit mentally unbalanced.

I wish also to thank my long-time friends and latter year employers Mike and Charlie Ebersberger of Angler's Sport Center, who kept me on staff for some twenty-odd years on a part time basis. This gave me access to beer and bait money plus a massive amount of angler feedback on the ecological wealth of the Bay and its many species as well as a first hand look at the tackle, equipment and strategies to catch anything that swam in our neighborhoods. I've had a fortunate life indeed in one of nature's richest and largest estuaries on the planet.

Thanks as well to my inlaws, Richard and Judy Barrett, for their support in making this book a reality. And designer Suzanne Shelden who gave this book its good looks.

Last but far from the least I wish to thank Sandra Olivetti Martin of *Bay Weekly* newspaper (and now New Bay Books, my publisher) who nurtured my career in outdoor journalism for over thirteen years and gave my life some form of discipline, otherwise sorely lacking.

I hope everyone can manage to be as lucky as I've been.

www.ingramcontent.com/pod-product-compliance
Lightning Source LLC
Chambersburg PA
CBHW070033030426
42335CB00017B/2407